Table of Contents

Introduction

- Why Process Improvement is Essential

Part I: Core Process Improvement Techniques

Chapter 1: DMAIC
- A Structured Approach to Reducing Scrap from the Extruder Lines by Identifying the Root Cause

Chapter 2: The 80/20 Rule (Pareto Principle)
- Focusing on the Most Impactful Problems

Chapter 3: A3 Problem Solving
- A Visual Approach to Problem Solving

Chapter 4: DPMA (Design Process Maturity Assessment)
- Evaluating Process Maturity

Chapter 5: Standard Deviation
- Understanding Process Variability

Part II: Tools for Error Reduction and Waste Elimination

Chapter 6: Poka-Yoke
- Error-Proofing for Process Reliability

Chapter 7: D.O.W.N.T.I.M.E.
- The 8 Common Forms of Waste in Lean Manufacturing

Chapter 8: Key Performance Indicators (KPIs)
- Measuring and Managing Performance

Chapter 9: The 5 Whys
- A Simple and Effective Root Cause Analysis Tool

Part III: Workflow Management and Lean Production

Chapter 10: Defects Per Million Opportunities (DPMO) – Measuring Process Quality in Six Sigma

Chapter 11: Kanban System
- A Visual Approach to Workflow Management

Chapter 12: SMED (Single-Minute Exchange of Dies)
- Reducing Changeover Time for Maximum Efficiency

Chapter 13: Just-In-Time (JIT) Production
- Maximizing Efficiency and Reducing Waste

Part IV: Standardization and Continuous Improvement

Chapter 14: Standard Operating Procedures (SOPs)
- Establishing Consistency and Quality in Manufacturing

Chapter 15: Kaizen
- The Path to Continuous Improvement in Manufacturing

Practical Application
Scenario: Continuous Improvement in Action at Polyethylene Pipe Manufacturing
- A Lean Journey

A Comprehensive Guide to Problem Solving and Process Improvement in Manufacturing

Introduction: Why Process Improvement is Essential

In the world of manufacturing and business, improving processes, reducing waste, and solving problems efficiently are critical to staying competitive. Many tools and methodologies have been developed to help companies systematically address problems and achieve excellence in operations. In this training, we will cover several key methodologies and tools, including:

- **DMAIC**: A structured, data-driven problem-solving method from Six Sigma.
- **The 80/20 Rule (Pareto Principle)**: A focus on the most impactful causes of problems.
- **A3 Problem Solving**: A visual problem-solving tool used in Lean management.
- **DPMA (Design Process Maturity Assessment)**: A tool for evaluating process maturity.
- **Standard Deviation**: A statistical measure of process variability.
- **Poka-Yoke**: A technique for preventing errors and defects.
- **8 Common Forms of Waste (D.O.W.N.T.I.M.E.)**: A Lean tool for identifying and eliminating waste.

We'll also draw on the insights of innovators like **W. Edwards Deming**, a key figure in quality management, and **Vilfredo Pareto**, whose work on the Pareto Principle shaped modern process improvement.

1. DMAIC: A Structured Approach to Problem Solving

The **DMAIC** process, central to **Lean Six Sigma**, provides a structured approach to problem-solving. The steps are **Define, Measure, Analyze, Improve**, and **Control**.

Key Innovator: W. Edwards Deming

W. Edwards Deming was one of the pioneers of quality management and introduced the **PDCA (Plan-Do-Check-Act)** cycle, which is closely related to DMAIC. His teachings on statistical process control and continuous improvement laid the foundation for Lean Six Sigma.

Define Phase:

In the **Define** phase, the problem is clearly articulated, and project goals are set.

- **Tools**:
  - **Project Charter**: A document outlining the project's scope, objectives, timeline, and team members.
  - **Voice of the Customer (VOC)**: Captures feedback from customers to ensure the problem-solving effort is aligned with their needs.
  - **SIPOC Diagram**: A high-level process map showing **Suppliers, Inputs, Process, Outputs, and Customers**.

Example: In a manufacturing environment, the problem could be "excessive scrap rates due to defects in polyethylene pipe production." The goal could be to reduce scrap rates from 10% to 2% within 6 months.

Measure Phase:

In the **Measure** phase, data is collected to establish a baseline and quantify the problem.

- **Tools**:
  - **Process Mapping**: A detailed flowchart that visualizes the current process.
  - **Data Collection Plan**: A systematic approach to gathering process data (e.g., defect rates, cycle times).
  - **Pareto Charts**: These charts help prioritize issues by showing which problems account for most of the waste or defects.

    Example: Collect data on defect types (e.g., uneven wall thickness or surface imperfections) and measure how often they occur. Use a Pareto Chart to see which defects contribute most to the scrap.

Analyze Phase:

In the **Analyze** phase, the root causes of the problem are identified.

- **Tools**:
  - **Root Cause Analysis**: Techniques like the **5 Whys** and **Fishbone Diagrams (Ishikawa Diagrams)** help identify underlying causes.
  - **Pareto Analysis**: Prioritizes the root causes contributing the most to the problem.

    Example: By asking "Why?" several times, you might discover that uneven pipe thickness is caused by fluctuating die temperatures.

Improve Phase:

In the **Improve** phase, solutions are developed and implemented.

- **Tools:**
  - **Brainstorming**: To generate potential solutions.
  - **Pilot Testing**: A small-scale test of the solution before full implementation.
  - **Poka-Yoke**: Introduce mistake-proofing techniques to eliminate errors.

Example: Install an automated temperature control system on the extruder lines to stabilize die temperatures and reduce defects.

Control Phase:

In the **Control** phase, improvements are sustained over time.

- **Tools:**
  - **Control Charts**: Track process performance and alert operators when variations occur.
  - **Standard Operating Procedures (SOPs)**: Document the improved process to ensure consistency.

Example: Use a **control chart** to monitor scrap rates and ensure the improvements (e.g., temperature control system) are maintained.

2. The 80/20 Rule (Pareto Principle): Focus on the Most Impactful Problems

The **80/20 Rule**, also known as the **Pareto Principle**, was introduced by **Vilfredo Pareto**, an Italian economist, in 1896. He observed that **80% of outcomes**

often come from 20% of causes. This principle is critical in problem-solving because it helps focus efforts on the most significant issues.

Pareto Charts:

A **Pareto Chart** is a bar chart that shows which factors contribute the most to a problem. It helps visualize the **vital few** (the 20%) that cause **80% of the problems**.

Example: In a factory, you might find that **80% of defects** come from just **two extruder lines** or that **80% of downtime** is caused by **20% of the equipment**. By addressing these key areas, you can significantly reduce defects and waste.

3. A3 Problem Solving: Visual Problem-Solving Tool

The **A3 Problem Solving** method is a Lean tool that uses a single sheet of paper (A3 size) to visually outline a problem, analysis, and proposed solution. It is a concise way to communicate problem-solving efforts and was popularized by **Toyota**.

Key Innovator: Taiichi Ohno

Taiichi Ohno, the father of the **Toyota Production System (TPS)**, introduced A3 Problem Solving as part of Toyota's continuous improvement culture.

Key Components of an A3 Report:

1. **Problem Statement**: Clearly define the issue.
2. **Current Situation**: Outline the current process and its inefficiencies.

3. **Root Cause Analysis**: Use tools like the 5 Whys to determine the root causes.
4. **Proposed Solutions**: Suggest and evaluate possible solutions.
5. **Action Plan**: Develop a step-by-step plan to implement the solution.
6. **Follow-up**: Monitor the results after implementation.

Example: If the problem is excessive defects, the A3 could show the **current scrap rates**, the root cause (e.g., poor die maintenance), and the solution (e.g., introduce a maintenance schedule for die equipment).

4. DPMA (Design Process Maturity Assessment): Evaluate Process Maturity

DPMA (Design Process Maturity Assessment) is a method for evaluating how mature and robust a process is. The idea is to assess how well-defined and repeatable a process is, and how effectively it meets business needs.

Process Maturity Levels:

1. **Initial (Ad-hoc)**: The process is unstructured and chaotic.
2. **Managed**: Basic project management controls are in place.
3. **Defined**: The process is standardized across the organization.
4. **Quantitatively Managed**: Metrics are used to control the process.
5. **Optimized**: Continuous improvement is embedded in the process.

Example: Assess the extrusion process in your factory. Is it standardized and consistently followed? If not, what areas need to be improved for higher maturity?

5. Standard Deviation: Understanding Process Variability

Standard Deviation is a statistical measure that quantifies the amount of variability or spread in a set of data. In manufacturing, it's important because **low variability** means the process is consistent, whereas **high variability** indicates the process may be out of control.

Key Innovator: Karl Pearson

Karl Pearson introduced the concept of **Standard Deviation** in the 1890s, and it has since become a fundamental tool in process control and quality management.

Control Charts:

A **Control Chart** tracks data over time and helps determine whether the process is stable. **Standard Deviation** is used to set control limits, so you can identify when the process is going out of control.

Example: In the extrusion process, you could track the **diameter of pipes**. If the diameter varies too much, it may indicate a problem with the extruder. Monitoring **standard deviations** allows you to detect when variability is increasing.

6. Poka-Yoke: Error-Proofing

Poka-Yoke, a Japanese term meaning "mistake-proofing," was introduced by **Shigeo Shingo**, an industrial engineer who worked at Toyota. The goal is to prevent errors from occurring by **designing processes or systems that automatically stop mistakes**.

Types of Poka-Yoke:

1. **Prevention Poka-Yoke**: Prevent mistakes from happening in the first place.
2. **Detection Poka-Yoke**: Detect and correct mistakes before they become defects.

Example: In the extruder line, a **Poka-Yoke** solution might involve installing sensors that automatically shut down the machine if the temperature goes out of range, preventing defects caused by overheating.

7. D.O.W.N.T.I.M.E: The 8 Common Forms of Waste in Lean Manufacturing

In Lean manufacturing, waste is any activity that does not add value to the customer. The acronym **D.O.W.N.T.I.M.E.** represents the **8 Common Forms of Waste**:

1. **D**efects: Producing defective products that require rework.
   - **Example**: Defective polyethylene pipes due to inconsistent thickness.
2. **O**verproduction: Producing more than is needed, leading to excess inventory.

- - **Example**: Manufacturing excess pipes before customer demand warrants it.
3. **Waiting**: Idle time when products or employees are waiting for the next step.
   - **Example**: Machines idle during manual die adjustments.
4. **Non-Utilized Talent**: Not using employees' skills to their fullest potential.
   - **Example**: Operators performing manual tasks that could be automated.
5. **Transportation**: Unnecessary movement of products or materials.
   - **Example**: Moving materials inefficiently between workstations.
6. **Inventory**: Holding excess raw materials or finished products.
   - **Example**: Excess polyethylene pellets stored due to overproduction.
7. **Motion**: Unnecessary movements of workers or machines.
   - **Example**: Operators walking long distances to retrieve tools.
8. **Extra Processing**: Performing more work than is necessary.
   - **Example**: Reworking defective pipes due to poor-quality control.

Conclusion: Integrating Problem-Solving Methods for Continuous Improvement

By understanding and using these methodologies, your team can continuously improve processes, reduce waste, and solve problems more effectively.

- **DMAIC** provides a structured approach to process improvement.
- **The 80/20 Rule** helps focus on the most impactful areas.
- **A3 Problem Solving** offers a visual, concise way to communicate problem-solving efforts.
- **DPMA** allows you to assess how mature your processes are.
- **Standard Deviation** helps monitor process consistency.

- **Poka-Yoke** prevents errors and defects before they happen.
- **D.O.W.N.T.I.M.E.** helps you identify and eliminate the most common forms of waste.

Drawing inspiration from pioneers like **W. Edwards Deming**, **Vilfredo Pareto**, and **Shigeo Shingo**, your organization can embed a culture of continuous improvement and problem-solving to drive operational excellence.

Chapter 1: DMAIC – A Structured Approach to Reducing Scrap from the Extruder Lines by Identifying the Root Cause

Introduction to DMAIC

The **DMAIC process** is a structured, systematic approach to solving problems in a way that identifies and addresses the root cause of an issue. When scrap rates are high in a manufacturing process, it's not always immediately clear **why** this is happening. In this chapter, we'll walk through how to apply DMAIC to an unknown problem—specifically, the challenge of **high scrap rates** on the extruder lines in a **polyethylene pipe manufacturing factory**. Through the DMAIC process, the team will eventually discover that **temperatures are too high** on the extruder lines, causing most of the defects.

Define Phase: Clearly Identifying the Problem

Since the root cause (high temperatures) is not yet known, the first step in DMAIC is to clearly define the **symptoms** of the problem and set a project goal.

1. Problem Statement

The team notices that the **scrap rate** on the extruder lines is unusually high, leading to wasted material, increased costs, and delays in production. However, they do not yet know what's causing the scrap. They only know that the **defects** are making the polyethylene pipes unusable.

- **Problem Statement Example**: "The scrap rate on extruder lines 1 and 2 is 12%, which is significantly higher than the industry standard of 2%. The goal is to reduce the scrap rate to 2% within 6 months."

2. Project Charter

A **Project Charter** is created to formalize the problem-solving effort, providing clear objectives, scope, timeline, and team members.

- **Scope**: Focus on extruder lines 1 and 2, where the most scrap is being generated.
- **Goal**: Reduce scrap from 12% to 2% by identifying and addressing the root cause.
- **Timeline**: The team will complete the Define phase in 1 week, Measure phase in 2 weeks, Analyze phase in 2 weeks, etc.
- **Team Members**: The team will include extruder operators, quality control staff, engineers, and maintenance personnel.

3. Voice of the Customer (VOC)

Gathering feedback from **customers** and **internal stakeholders** helps define the symptoms of the problem. **External customers** are reporting that the pipes are arriving with defects like **brittleness**, **uneven thickness**, and **surface imperfections**. **Internal customers**, such as quality control teams and machine operators, report frequent issues with defective pipes that lead to scrap and rework.

- **External VOC Example**: "We've had to reject entire batches of pipes due to their inconsistency and brittleness. These pipes cannot be used in construction."

- **Internal VOC Example**: "We are constantly seeing defects in the pipes coming off extruder lines 1 and 2, especially after die changes."

4. SIPOC Diagram

A **SIPOC Diagram** (Suppliers, Inputs, Process, Outputs, Customers) helps the team map out the process and identify where problems might be occurring.

- **Suppliers**: Polyethylene pellet suppliers, equipment suppliers.
- **Inputs**: Polyethylene pellets, machine settings, temperature controls.
- **Process**: Load → Heat and Melt → Extrude → Cool → Cut → Inspect.
- **Outputs**: Polyethylene pipes (including defective products).
- **Customers**: End users, construction companies.

Measure Phase: Gathering Data to Quantify the Problem

In the **Measure** phase, the team starts gathering data to better understand the process and the current extent of the problem. At this stage, the **root cause** is still unknown, so the focus is on collecting enough data to analyze potential causes later.

1. Document the Process

The team creates a **process map** or **flowchart** to document each step of the extrusion process. This allows them to visualize where problems might be occurring and what needs to be measured.

- **Process Map Example**:
1. **Loading**: Polyethylene pellets are loaded into the extruder.
2. **Heating**: Pellets are melted into a liquid form.
3. **Extrusion**: The molten material is forced through a die to form the pipe shape.
4. **Cooling**: The pipe is cooled in a water bath to solidify.
5. **Cutting**: The pipe is cut into segments.
6. **Inspection**: Finished pipes are inspected for defects like **brittleness** and **uneven wall thickness**.

2. Data Collection Plan

The team develops a **data collection plan** to gather baseline data on defect rates, machine settings, and environmental factors (e.g., temperatures, pressure).

- **Metrics to Collect**:
  - **Scrap Rate**: Currently at 12%.
  - **Defect Types**: Categorize defects (brittleness, thickness variation, surface imperfections).
  - **Temperature Readings**: Collect temperature data from different sections of the extruder (e.g., die, barrel).
  - **Production Output**: Track how many pipes are produced per shift and how many are scrapped.

Example Data Collection Plan:

  - **Duration**: Collect data over 2 weeks on extruder lines 1 and 2.
  - **Key Measurements**: Record temperature every hour, log the number of defective pipes per shift, and document the types of defects.

3. Pareto Chart

The team uses a **Pareto Chart** to prioritize which defects are contributing most to the scrap. According to the **Pareto Principle (80/20 Rule)**, most of the problems are caused by a few factors.

- **Example Pareto Chart**: The chart shows that **85% of defects** are due to two main issues: **brittleness** (50%) and **uneven thickness** (35%).

4. Control Charts

The team sets up **Control Charts** to track **temperature fluctuations** and **scrap rates** over time. If there are variations in temperature, this could point to an equipment or process issue.

Analyze Phase: Identifying the Root Cause of High Scrap Rates

The **Analyze** phase is where the team examines the data collected in the Measure phase to figure out **why** the defects are happening. At this point, they still don't know that **high temperatures** are the root cause.

1. Root Cause Analysis (Fishbone Diagram)

A **Fishbone Diagram** is used to explore possible causes of the high scrap rate. The team investigates various factors, including **People, Process, Equipment, Materials,** and **Environment**.

- **Fishbone Diagram Example**:
  - **People**: Operators not properly trained on temperature settings.

- **Process**: Inconsistent production cycle or irregular maintenance of equipment.
- **Equipment**: Possible issues with the extruder's temperature control system.
- **Materials**: Low-quality polyethylene pellets requiring different temperature settings.
- **Environment**: Ambient factory temperature affecting the extrusion process.

2. 5 Whys Technique

The team uses the **5 Whys** technique to dig deeper into the **root causes** of the scrap. They start by asking, "Why are the pipes defective?"

- **Example 5 Whys**:
  - **Why are the pipes brittle?** – Because the material is overheating during extrusion.
  - **Why is the material overheating?** – The temperature on the extruder is too high.
  - **Why is the temperature too high?** – The temperature control system is malfunctioning.
  - **Why is the temperature control system malfunctioning?** – It hasn't been calibrated properly in over a year.
  - **Why hasn't it been calibrated?** – There's no preventive maintenance schedule in place for this system.

3. Data Correlation

After analyzing the data, the team finds a **strong correlation** between **higher temperatures** and the **defective pipes**. When the temperature exceeds a certain threshold (e.g., 220°C), the scrap rate spikes, and the types of defects (brittleness and thickness variation) match those observed.

Improve Phase: Implementing Solutions to Fix the High Temperature Issue

Now that the team knows the **root cause** is **high temperatures** on the extruder lines, the **Improve** phase focuses on creating and implementing solutions to address this problem.

1. Brainstorm Solutions

The team generates potential solutions for reducing the high temperatures and preventing defects.

Example Solutions:

1. **Install a new temperature control system**: Upgrade to a system with automatic calibration and more precise temperature regulation.
2. **Implement a preventive maintenance schedule**: Regularly calibrate the temperature control system to ensure consistent operation.
3. **Train operators**: Teach operators how to adjust temperature settings appropriately based on the material being used.

2. Pilot Testing

Before rolling out the solution factory-wide, conduct a **pilot test** on one extruder line to assess its effectiveness.

- **Pilot Example**: The team installs a new temperature control system on **Extruder Line 1** and monitors it for 2 weeks. They track whether the system keeps temperatures within the optimal range and whether it reduces the number of defective pipes.

3. Implement Poka-Yoke (Mistake-Proofing)

The team applies **Poka-Yoke** to prevent further temperature-related errors.

- **Poka-Yoke Example**: A **temperature sensor** is installed that automatically shuts down the extruder if the temperature exceeds the set limit (e.g., 220°C). This ensures that no pipes are produced under suboptimal conditions.

Control Phase: Sustaining the Improvements

In the **Control** phase, the team ensures that the improvements made during the Improve phase are **maintained** over time to prevent the issue from reoccurring.

1. Control Charts

The team uses **Control Charts** to continuously monitor the temperature on the extruder lines, ensuring that it stays within the desired range (e.g., 200°C–220°C).

- **Control Chart Example**: If the temperature drifts out of this range, the control chart will trigger an alert, prompting the operator to check the system.

2. Standard Operating Procedures (SOPs)

The team creates new **Standard Operating Procedures (SOPs)** that include steps for regular calibration of the temperature control system and guidelines for setting optimal temperatures.

- **SOP Example**: The SOP includes a detailed guide for operators on how to maintain the correct temperature settings, perform routine checks, and log any system deviations.

3. Preventive Maintenance Schedule

A **preventive maintenance schedule** is established to ensure that the temperature control system is regularly calibrated and serviced.

Through the DMAIC process, the team was able to systematically uncover that **high temperatures** were the root cause of the high scrap rates on the extruder lines. By implementing solutions such as a new temperature control system and mistake-proofing mechanisms, the factory was able to reduce its scrap rate from **12% to 2%**. Regular monitoring and a preventive maintenance schedule ensure that the improvements are sustained over time.

This chapter has demonstrated how DMAIC can be used to **solve problems step-by-step**, even when the root cause is not immediately known. By following this structured approach, manufacturing teams can tackle complex issues and achieve long-lasting results.

Chapter 2: The 80/20 Rule (Pareto Principle) – Focusing on the Most Impactful Problems

Introduction to the 80/20 Rule (Pareto Principle)

The **80/20 Rule**, also known as the **Pareto Principle**, is a powerful tool for prioritizing efforts and resources to solve problems effectively. The principle is based on the observation that **80% of the effects come from 20% of the causes**. In other words, in many situations, a small number of causes are responsible for the majority of problems.

This concept was first introduced by **Vilfredo Pareto**, an Italian economist, who noticed that **80% of Italy's wealth was owned by 20% of the population**. Over time, this principle has been widely applied in business, economics, and manufacturing to focus improvement efforts on the most significant factors.

In this chapter, we will use the **Pareto Principle** to analyze and prioritize problems in a **polyethylene pipe manufacturing factory**, where **high scrap rates** are being observed on the extruder lines. As the team uncovers the **root cause** of the high scrap rate through the **DMAIC process**, the 80/20 Rule will help the team focus on the most impactful factors—ultimately leading to the discovery that **high temperatures** are responsible for the majority of the defects.

The Basics of the 80/20 Rule

The **80/20 Rule** applies broadly, but in the context of manufacturing, it typically looks like this:

- **80% of defects come from 20% of the causes.**
- **80% of waste is generated by 20% of processes.**
- **80% of downtime is caused by 20% of equipment.**

The principle encourages focusing on the **vital few**—the 20% of causes that lead to most of the problems—while avoiding getting distracted by the **trivial many**—the 80% of minor causes that only lead to a small portion of the problem.

Applying the 80/20 Rule to Reduce Scrap on the Extruder Lines

In the case of the polyethylene pipe manufacturing factory, the problem is that the **scrap rate** on the extruder lines is too high (12%). The challenge is to identify which specific causes are responsible for the majority of these defects. The **Pareto Principle** will help the team focus on the **critical few** factors, which, when addressed, will yield the greatest reduction in scrap.

Step 1: Collecting Data on Defects and Scrap Rates

To apply the 80/20 Rule, the team first needs to collect data on the defects and scrap rates. Since they do not yet know that **high temperatures** are the root cause of the problem, the team needs to record every possible variable involved in the production process to see where the biggest issues are.

Key Data Points to Collect:

- **Types of defects**: Brittleness, uneven thickness, surface imperfections, etc.
- **Frequency of defects**: How often each type of defect occurs per shift, per machine, or per batch.
- **Scrap rates**: Measure the number of defective pipes relative to the total produced, broken down by shift and machine.
- **Other factors**: Record machine settings (e.g., temperature, pressure), operator actions, and environmental factors (e.g., humidity, factory temperature).

The team records this data over a two-week period, across all shifts and machines. They collect information on every defect that occurs on **extruder lines 1 and 2**, where the highest scrap rates are observed.

Step 2: Creating a Pareto Chart to Visualize the Problem

Once the data is collected, the team can now create a **Pareto Chart** to identify which defects are contributing the most to the scrap. A **Pareto Chart** is a bar graph that helps visualize the **frequency** of each defect type and shows how much each defect contributes to the overall scrap rate.

How to Create a Pareto Chart:

1. **List all defects**: The team lists all the different types of defects (e.g., brittleness, uneven thickness, surface imperfections).
2. **Sort defects by frequency**: The defects are sorted from the most frequent to the least frequent.

3. **Calculate cumulative percentage**: The team calculates the percentage of total defects that each type represents, then adds up these percentages cumulatively.
4. **Create a bar graph**: The defects are displayed as bars, with the most frequent defect on the left. A line chart can be added to show the cumulative percentage of defects.

Example Pareto Chart:

The team's **Pareto Chart** might look something like this:

Defect Type	Frequency (number of occurrences)	% of Total Defects	Cumulative %
Brittleness	500	50%	50%
Uneven Thickness	350	35%	85%
Surface Imperfections	100	10%	95%
Other Defects	50	5%	100%

From this chart, the team can clearly see that **85% of the defects** come from just two causes: **brittleness** (50%) and **uneven thickness** (35%).

Step 3: Analyzing the Pareto Chart to Focus on the Critical Few

With the Pareto Chart complete, the team now understands that their **scrap problem** is largely caused by **brittleness** and **uneven thickness**. According to the **Pareto Principle**, focusing their efforts on reducing these two types of defects will have the most significant impact on reducing the overall scrap rate.

Focusing on Brittleness and Uneven Thickness:

- **Brittleness**: This defect makes the pipes weak and prone to cracking. The team now needs to investigate why the pipes are brittle—this could be due to issues with material quality, overheating during extrusion, or improper cooling.
- **Uneven Thickness**: Pipes with inconsistent wall thickness cannot meet industry standards and are rejected by customers. This defect may be related to improper extrusion pressure, inconsistent temperature during extrusion, or worn-out machinery.

The **80/20 Rule** helps the team realize that they shouldn't spread their efforts thin by addressing all types of defects equally. Instead, by focusing on **brittleness** and **uneven thickness**, they can make the most progress with the least effort.

Step 4: Digging Deeper into the Most Common Defects

Now that the team has used the Pareto Chart to identify **brittleness** and **uneven thickness** as the most common and impactful defects, they can begin investigating the **root causes** of these issues.

Using Root Cause Analysis: To further investigate, the team uses tools such as the **5 Whys** and a **Fishbone Diagram** to figure out why these defects are occurring.

- **Brittleness**: The team starts with brittleness, asking "Why are the pipes brittle?" After using the **5 Whys** technique, they trace the issue back to **high**

temperatures in the extruder line. High temperatures are causing the material to overheat, which makes the pipes brittle once they cool.
- **Uneven Thickness**: The team investigates uneven thickness next. Using a **Fishbone Diagram**, they explore potential causes related to **people, processes, equipment, and materials**. Again, they find that **inconsistent temperature control** is a major factor—temperature fluctuations during extrusion are leading to uneven material flow, which causes the walls of the pipes to vary in thickness.

Step 5: Implementing Solutions to Address the Vital Few Causes

Now that the team has identified **high temperatures** as the root cause of both **brittleness** and **uneven thickness**, they can move on to the **Improve phase** of DMAIC, implementing solutions that will focus on these critical areas.

Example Solutions:

1. **Temperature Control System**: Install a more advanced temperature control system to ensure consistent temperature during extrusion.
2. **Preventive Maintenance**: Implement a preventive maintenance schedule to regularly check and calibrate the temperature control system.
3. **Operator Training**: Train operators on how to monitor and adjust temperature settings to ensure they stay within optimal ranges.

By focusing on these **vital few** factors—temperature control—the team will be able to address **85% of the defects**, dramatically reducing the scrap rate.

Step 6: Monitoring and Sustaining Improvements

Finally, the team needs to **monitor** the changes to ensure they are effective over time. They will continue to track the **scrap rate** and **temperature control data** using **Control Charts** to make sure the improvements are maintained.

Conclusion: The Power of the 80/20 Rule

The **80/20 Rule** (Pareto Principle) provided the team with a clear focus. By using a **Pareto Chart**, they discovered that **85% of the defects** were caused by just two factors: **brittleness** and **uneven thickness**. Further analysis revealed that **high temperatures** were the root cause of both issues.

By focusing on this **vital 20%**, the team was able to make targeted improvements, installing a new temperature control system and training operators to monitor and adjust temperature settings. This focus allowed them to achieve the greatest possible reduction in scrap with the least amount of effort.

This chapter has demonstrated how the **80/20 Rule** helps teams focus their problem-solving efforts on the most impactful areas, ensuring faster, more efficient results in manufacturing and other processes.

Chapter 3: A3 Problem Solving – A Visual Approach to Problem Solving

Introduction to A3 Problem Solving

A3 Problem Solving is a structured, visual method used in **Lean manufacturing** to address problems and communicate solutions concisely. The term "A3" comes from the size of the paper used for the report (A3 paper, 11.7 x 16.5 inches), but the real value of A3 problem-solving lies in its **systematic approach** to breaking down complex problems into understandable parts. It was popularized by **Toyota**, where it became an integral part of their continuous improvement culture, known as the **Toyota Production System (TPS)**.

A3 problem-solving encourages **root cause analysis**, **data-driven decision making**, and **team collaboration**, all while being documented on a single piece of paper. In this chapter, we will explore how the **A3 Problem Solving** method can be applied to a specific manufacturing issue: **high scrap rates on extruder lines in a polyethylene pipe manufacturing factory**. Through the A3 process, we'll follow the team as they uncover that the **high temperatures** on the extruder lines are the root cause of their problem.

The A3 Template: Overview of Sections

The A3 report is divided into several sections that guide the problem-solving process. These sections include:

1. **Background**: Context for the problem.

2. **Current Condition**: Description of the current problem and data.
3. **Goal/Target**: What you aim to achieve.
4. **Root Cause Analysis**: Identifying the root cause of the problem.
5. **Countermeasures**: Proposed solutions to address the root cause.
6. **Implementation Plan**: Steps for implementing the solutions.
7. **Follow-up/Results**: Monitoring results after implementation.

Now, let's walk through how the team in the **polyethylene pipe manufacturing factory** applies A3 Problem Solving to reduce scrap rates and uncover the root cause of their problem.

Step 1: Background – Framing the Problem

The **Background** section provides context for the issue and explains why solving it is important. In this case, the factory is experiencing a high scrap rate on the extruder lines, but the exact cause is unknown.

Example Background:

- **Context**: The factory has seen an increase in defective polyethylene pipes produced on **Extruder Lines 1 and 2**. The scrap rate has reached **12%**, well above the industry standard of **2%**, leading to higher material costs and reduced efficiency.
- **Impact**: The high scrap rate is costing the company an additional $50,000 per month in wasted materials and delayed orders.

A3 Report - Background Example:

- **Problem**: "Scrap rates on extruder lines 1 and 2 have risen to 12%, significantly impacting production efficiency and increasing material costs."
- **Importance**: "This issue must be addressed to reduce costs, meet production targets, and maintain customer satisfaction."

Step 2: Current Condition – Understanding the Problem with Data

The **Current Condition** section describes the **current state** of the process using data. The goal is to clearly define the problem, supported by **quantitative data** such as scrap rates, defect types, and production metrics. This helps everyone involved understand the scale and specifics of the problem.

Example Current Condition:

- **Scrap Rate**: 12% of pipes produced on extruder lines 1 and 2 are being scrapped due to defects such as **brittleness, uneven wall thickness**, and **surface imperfections**.
- **Defect Types**: The team records the types of defects over a two-week period and finds that **85% of defects** are due to brittleness (50%) and uneven thickness (35%).
- **Observations**: Operators report that defects seem to occur more frequently during die changes and when extruder temperatures fluctuate.

A3 Report - Current Condition Example:

- **Scrap Rate**: "Currently, 12% of pipes on extruder lines 1 and 2 are scrapped due to defects."

- **Defects**: "85% of defects are related to **brittleness** (50%) and **uneven wall thickness** (35%)."
- **Observation**: "Defects seem to be linked to temperature fluctuations during production."

Step 3: Goal/Target – Setting a Clear Objective

In this section, the team defines the **specific goal** or **target** they want to achieve. This target should be **measurable** and **time-bound**.

Example Goal/Target:

- **Goal**: Reduce the scrap rate from 12% to **2%** on extruder lines 1 and 2 within the next **6 months**.
- **Additional Goal**: Stabilize the temperature control system to prevent fluctuations that cause defects.

A3 Report - Goal/Target Example:

- **Target**: "Reduce the scrap rate to 2% by optimizing temperature controls on extruder lines 1 and 2 within 6 months."

Step 4: Root Cause Analysis – Identifying the Real Problem

The **Root Cause Analysis** section is where the team digs deeper to find out **why** the defects are occurring. At this point, the root cause is still unknown, but through careful investigation using tools like the **5 Whys** and a **Fishbone Diagram**, the team identifies the underlying issue—**high temperatures** during the extrusion process.

1. Fishbone Diagram

The team uses a **Fishbone Diagram** (also called an **Ishikawa Diagram**) to brainstorm possible causes of the high scrap rate. They consider factors such as **People**, **Process**, **Equipment**, **Materials**, and **Environment**.

Example Fishbone Diagram:

Cause Categories	Potential Causes
People	Inadequate operator training on temperature settings
Process	Inconsistent procedures during die changes
Equipment	Faulty temperature control system
Materials	Low-quality polyethylene requiring higher temps
Environment	External heat impacting machine settings

2. The 5 Whys Technique

To get to the root cause, the team uses the **5 Whys** technique:

- **Why are the pipes brittle?** – Because the material is overheating during extrusion.
- **Why is the material overheating?** – Because the extruder temperature is too high.
- **Why is the extruder temperature too high?** – The temperature control system is malfunctioning.
- **Why is the temperature control system malfunctioning?** – It hasn't been properly calibrated.

- **Why hasn't it been calibrated?** – There is no preventive maintenance schedule in place for temperature control calibration.

Through this investigation, the team identifies the **root cause: The temperature control system is malfunctioning, leading to temperatures that are too high during the extrusion process.**

A3 Report - Root Cause Analysis Example:

- **Root Cause**: "The high scrap rate is caused by **overheating** during the extrusion process due to a **malfunctioning temperature control system.**"

Step 5: Countermeasures – Proposing Solutions to Fix the Problem

The **Countermeasures** section outlines **potential solutions** (also called countermeasures) to address the root cause of the problem. These solutions should focus on eliminating or controlling the root cause to reduce defects.

Example Countermeasures:

1. **Install a new temperature control system**: Replace the malfunctioning system with one that provides more precise control.
2. **Preventive Maintenance**: Implement a regular calibration schedule for the temperature control system.
3. **Operator Training**: Train operators to monitor and adjust the temperature settings to maintain optimal extrusion conditions.
4. **Poka-Yoke Solution**: Install a fail-safe sensor that shuts down the extruder if the temperature exceeds a certain threshold.

A3 Report - Countermeasures Example:

- **Solution 1**: "Install a new, advanced temperature control system on extruder lines 1 and 2."
- **Solution 2**: "Implement a preventive maintenance schedule for regular calibration of the temperature control system."
- **Solution 3**: "Train operators on how to maintain and adjust temperature settings based on material type and production conditions."

Step 6: Implementation Plan – Putting Solutions into Action

The **Implementation Plan** section lays out the **steps** for carrying out the solutions identified in the Countermeasures section. This plan includes who is responsible, what needs to be done, and when it will be completed.

Example Implementation Plan:

- **Step 1**: Purchase and install the new temperature control system (Responsible: Maintenance team, Timeline: 2 weeks).
- **Step 2**: Develop and implement the preventive maintenance schedule (Responsible: Process Engineer, Timeline: 1 week after installation).
- **Step 3**: Conduct operator training sessions on the new temperature control system (Responsible: Training Manager, Timeline: 1 week after installation).
- **Step 4**: Install Poka-Yoke sensors (Responsible: Engineering team, Timeline: 3 weeks).

A3 Report - Implementation Plan Example:

- **Timeline**: "The new temperature control system will be installed within 2 weeks, followed by operator training and calibration. Full implementation will be completed within 4 weeks."

Step 7: Follow-up and Results – Monitoring and Measuring Success

The **Follow-up/Results** section tracks the success of the implemented solutions. The team should measure **key metrics** (such as scrap rate and temperature stability) to ensure the countermeasures are working and to determine if further adjustments are needed.

Example Follow-up/Results:

- **Scrap Rate**: The scrap rate is monitored over a 3-month period. Within the first month of implementing the new temperature control system, the scrap rate drops from 12% to **3%**. By the end of the second month, it reaches the target of **2%**.
- **Temperature Stability**: Data from the new control system shows that temperature fluctuations have been eliminated, and the system maintains a consistent temperature throughout the extrusion process.
- **Operator Feedback**: Operators report that the new system is easy to use, and there have been no further incidents of overheating.

A3 Report - Follow-up Example:

- **Results**: "The scrap rate has been reduced to 2%, achieving the target within 3 months of implementing the new temperature control system and preventive maintenance schedule."

Conclusion: The Power of A3 Problem Solving

The **A3 Problem Solving** method provided a **clear, visual framework** for the team to identify, analyze, and solve the problem of **high scrap rates** on the extruder lines. By using structured tools like the **Fishbone Diagram** and **5 Whys**, the team was able to uncover the root cause—**high temperatures** due to a malfunctioning temperature control system.

They then developed and implemented effective **countermeasures**, resulting in a significant reduction in the scrap rate, improved process stability, and more efficient production.

A3 problem-solving is not only a tool for **problem resolution** but also a way to **engage teams** and **foster collaboration**. The concise format of an A3 report ensures that the entire problem-solving process—from the current condition to results—is clearly communicated and easy to follow.

This chapter illustrates the effectiveness of A3 in tackling real-world manufacturing problems and achieving long-term, sustainable improvements.

Chapter 4: DPMA (Design Process Maturity Assessment) – Evaluating Process Maturity

Introduction to DPMA (Design Process Maturity Assessment)

DPMA (Design Process Maturity Assessment) is a framework used to evaluate the **maturity** of processes within an organization. By understanding how mature a process is, a company can assess how well its processes are managed, standardized, and controlled, and how consistently they deliver reliable results. The goal of DPMA is to identify where a process stands on the **maturity scale** and what steps can be taken to improve it, ensuring that the processes are robust, optimized, and capable of producing high-quality outcomes with minimal variability.

Process maturity is critical in **manufacturing**, where **consistency**, **efficiency**, and **quality** are essential to achieving operational excellence. In this chapter, we'll use DPMA to assess the **extruder line process** in a **polyethylene pipe manufacturing factory**, where the problem of **high scrap rates** is observed. The assessment will help the team determine how mature their process is, leading to the discovery that the **temperature control system** is a key area that requires maturity improvements.

The Importance of Process Maturity in Manufacturing

A mature process is:

- **Consistent**: It produces the same results time and again, with minimal variation.
- **Controlled**: It has clear metrics, control mechanisms, and preventive measures.
- **Optimized**: It continuously evolves through improvement efforts.
- **Predictable**: It operates in a way that allows for forecasting outcomes accurately.

In contrast, an immature process may be:

- **Unpredictable**: Outcomes vary significantly from one batch to the next.
- **Uncontrolled**: There are few, if any, metrics to monitor performance.
- **Inefficient**: The process is prone to waste and defects, leading to unnecessary rework and material loss.

The 5 Levels of Process Maturity

DPMA evaluates processes across five levels of maturity, from **ad-hoc** to **optimized**. The goal is to move processes from low maturity (where results are unpredictable and inconsistent) to high maturity (where processes are controlled, predictable, and continuously improving).

Level 1: Initial (Ad-hoc)

- **Characteristics**: Processes are unstructured and reactive. Success depends on individual efforts, and results are inconsistent.
- **Example**: There is no formal temperature control system on the extruder lines. Operators manually adjust settings based on experience, leading to frequent fluctuations in temperature and scrap rates.

Level 2: Managed

- **Characteristics**: Basic process management is in place. Some repeatability exists, but the process is not well-documented or standardized.
- **Example**: The factory has a basic temperature control system, but it is outdated and lacks automated calibration. There are no preventive maintenance procedures to ensure that the system operates within acceptable limits.

Level 3: Defined

- **Characteristics**: Processes are documented and standardized. There is an understanding of the key metrics and inputs, but variations are not fully controlled.
- **Example**: The temperature control system is updated and calibrated periodically, but there is variability in how it is used by different operators. Standard operating procedures (SOPs) exist, but adherence is inconsistent.

Level 4: Quantitatively Managed

- **Characteristics**: Metrics are used to manage and control processes. Statistical methods are employed to ensure consistency and quality.
- **Example**: The temperature control system is fully automated and linked to a monitoring system that tracks real-time temperature data. Operators can view trends and deviations, and alerts are triggered when temperatures fall outside of the acceptable range.

Level 5: Optimized

- **Characteristics**: Continuous improvement is built into the process. The process is fully optimized, and predictive analytics are used to prevent issues before they occur.
- **Example**: The temperature control system is not only automated but also integrates with predictive maintenance tools. The system predicts when adjustments are needed based on data trends, preventing overheating and ensuring minimal defects.

Applying DPMA to the Polyethylene Pipe Manufacturing Process

In this example, the **extruder lines** are producing polyethylene pipes, but the process is plagued by a **high scrap rate**. Through the **DMAIC process**, the team discovered that the root cause of the high scrap rate was **fluctuating temperatures** during the extrusion process. Using DPMA, the team will assess the **maturity** of the extrusion process and identify where improvements need to be made to stabilize the temperature control system and reduce the scrap rate.

Step 1: Assessing the Current Process Maturity

Current State (Level 2: Managed)

- **Process Description**: The current process involves using an **outdated temperature control system** that requires frequent manual adjustments by operators. There are **no preventive maintenance procedures**, and **temperature fluctuations** occur often, leading to defects such as brittleness and uneven wall thickness.
- **Key Metrics**: The scrap rate is **12%**, which is far above the industry standard of 2%. The team collects temperature data and finds significant variability across shifts and operators.
- **Maturity Level**: The process is at **Level 2 (Managed)**. While the process exists and basic temperature controls are in place, it is largely **reactive** rather than proactive. There is **no formal system** in place for regular calibration, and the process relies heavily on individual operator experience.

Step 2: Identifying Gaps and Weaknesses

The DPMA assessment reveals several **gaps** in the extrusion process that are contributing to the high scrap rate:

1. **Lack of Process Control**: Temperature settings are adjusted manually, leading to inconsistencies across shifts. Operators rely on their personal judgment rather than clear guidelines or automatic systems.
2. **No Preventive Maintenance**: The temperature control system is not maintained or calibrated regularly, leading to gradual drift in temperature readings over time.

3. **Inconsistent Documentation**: There are no standardized procedures for setting or maintaining optimal temperatures during the extrusion process, and operator practices vary widely.
4. **No Metrics for Predictive Analysis**: The factory does not use metrics or data to predict temperature deviations or process failures before they occur.

Step 3: Moving Towards Higher Process Maturity

To move the extrusion process from **Level 2 (Managed)** to **Level 4 (Quantitatively Managed)** or **Level 5 (Optimized)**, the team must address the gaps identified in the assessment. The following steps outline how to improve process maturity.

1. Implement an Automated Temperature Control System (Moving to Level 3: Defined)

- **Goal**: Replace the manual temperature control system with an **automated system** that can maintain consistent temperature settings without operator intervention.
- **Action**: Install a new temperature control system with real-time monitoring and automated adjustments. Ensure the system can maintain temperatures within the acceptable range for the specific polyethylene material being extruded.
- **Benefit**: This will standardize temperature settings across all shifts and operators, reducing variability and improving product quality.

2. Establish Standard Operating Procedures (Moving to Level 3: Defined)

- **Goal**: Develop and document **SOPs** for the extrusion process, with a focus on temperature control, maintenance schedules, and defect detection.
- **Action**: Work with operators and engineers to document the **best practices** for maintaining temperature consistency. Ensure that SOPs are clearly communicated and that all operators are trained to follow them.
- **Benefit**: Consistent application of SOPs will reduce operator variability and ensure that the process is stable, regardless of who is running the equipment.

3. Introduce Preventive Maintenance (Moving to Level 4: Quantitatively Managed)

- **Goal**: Implement a **preventive maintenance schedule** for the temperature control system to ensure regular calibration and avoid equipment failure.
- **Action**: Create a maintenance schedule that includes **regular calibration** of the temperature control system, inspections of the extruder equipment, and replacement of worn parts.
- **Benefit**: Regular maintenance will prevent **temperature drift** and equipment failures, reducing the risk of defects and unplanned downtime.

4. Use Control Charts and Statistical Process Control (Moving to Level 4: Quantitatively Managed)

- **Goal**: Introduce **Statistical Process Control (SPC)** tools, such as **Control Charts**, to monitor and control temperature variability in real time.

- **Action**: Set up real-time **temperature monitoring** on the extruder lines. Use **control limits** to detect when temperatures deviate from the acceptable range and trigger alerts for operators.
- **Benefit**: This will allow the team to **proactively manage** the process by identifying deviations before they cause defects, keeping the process within controlled parameters.

5. Integrate Predictive Analytics (Moving to Level 5: Optimized)

- **Goal**: Incorporate **predictive analytics** to forecast temperature control system performance and predict potential issues before they lead to defects.
- **Action**: Collect historical data from the temperature control system and use **predictive models** to identify trends that may lead to process failures. Integrate this data with maintenance schedules to prevent failures before they happen.
- **Benefit**: Predictive analytics will allow the factory to move beyond reactive maintenance and **optimize** the process for maximum efficiency and minimum defects.

Step 4: Tracking Progress and Results

After implementing the steps to improve process maturity, the team must track progress to ensure that the extrusion process continues to mature.

1. Key Metrics to Track:

- **Scrap Rate**: The scrap rate should decrease as process maturity increases, moving from **12% to the target of 2%**.

- **Temperature Stability**: Measure the variability in temperature over time. A mature process will maintain consistent temperatures within a narrow range.
- **Defect Reduction**: Track the reduction in defects caused by high temperatures (e.g., brittleness and uneven thickness).

2. Monitoring Process Maturity:

Use **Process Audits** and **Key Performance Indicators (KPIs)** to continually assess the maturity level of the extrusion process. Regular audits will ensure that SOPs are followed, preventive maintenance is performed, and the temperature control system is functioning properly.

Conclusion: The Role of DPMA in Continuous Improvement

The **Design Process Maturity Assessment (DPMA)** provides a structured way to evaluate the maturity of manufacturing processes. By applying DPMA to the **extrusion process** in a polyethylene pipe manufacturing factory, the team was able to identify key weaknesses—such as **manual temperature control**, **lack of preventive maintenance**, and **inconsistent procedures**—that were leading to a high scrap rate.

Through systematic improvements, such as **automating temperature controls**, implementing **SOPs**, and using **Statistical Process Control (SPC)**, the team was able to move the process toward a higher level of maturity, leading to **greater consistency**, **lower scrap rates**, and **improved process stability**.As processes become more mature, they become **more predictable** and **optimized**, contributing to **better quality**, **reduced costs**, and **higher efficiency**. DPMA is an essential tool for companies looking to **evaluate**, **improve**, and **optimize** their processes over time, making it an integral part of the **continuous improvement** journey.

Chapter 5: Standard Deviation – Understanding Process Variability

Introduction to Standard Deviation in Manufacturing

Standard deviation is a key statistical tool used to measure the amount of **variation** or **dispersion** in a process. It tells us how much individual data points (like product dimensions, temperatures, or defect rates) differ from the average (mean) value. Understanding standard deviation is crucial in **process control**, particularly in manufacturing, where **consistency** and **precision** are critical to delivering high-quality products.

In this chapter, we will explore how **standard deviation** is used to assess and manage **process variability** in a **polyethylene pipe manufacturing factory**, specifically on the **extruder lines** where scrap rates are high. Through the use of standard deviation, the team will gain insight into the temperature variations during the extrusion process and how those variations impact the quality of the pipes being produced.

What is Standard Deviation?

Standard deviation measures the spread of data points around the mean. In manufacturing, this is useful for determining how much a process deviates from its target value and whether the variability is within acceptable limits.

- **Low standard deviation** means the data points are close to the mean, indicating a **consistent** process.
- **High standard deviation** means the data points are spread out over a wider range, indicating **high variability** and potential **inconsistencies** in the process.

Formula for Standard Deviation:

$$\sigma = \sqrt{\frac{1}{N}\sum_{i=1}^{N}(x_i - \mu)^2}$$

Where:

- σ = Standard deviation
- N = Number of data points
- x_i = Each individual data point
- μ = Mean (average) of the data points

Understanding the Formula for Standard Deviation

Standard deviation is a statistical measure used to quantify the amount of **variation** or **dispersion** in a set of data points. In the context of manufacturing, standard deviation helps measure the **variability** in a process—such as variations in product dimensions, temperature control, or defect rates—and assesses how consistent the process is over time.

A **low standard deviation** means that the data points are tightly clustered around the **mean**, indicating that the process is consistent. A **high standard deviation** means that the data points are spread out over a wider range, signaling that the process has a lot of variation, which could lead to quality issues.

I bet you thought I was going to leave it at the hard math!! Here's the simplified version.

Simplified Explanation of Standard Deviation for Easier Understanding

Standard Deviation is a way to measure **how spread out numbers are** from the average (or mean). In a manufacturing setting, it helps us understand whether our process is **consistent** or if the products have a lot of **variability**.

If the **standard deviation** is **low**, it means that most of the measurements are **close to the average**, and the process is likely stable. If the **standard deviation** is **high**, it means that the measurements are more **spread out**, and the process might have issues with consistency, leading to defects.

Breaking Down Standard Deviation in Simple Steps

To make this concept more understandable, let's break it into **five simple steps**:

Step 1: Find the Average (Mean)

First, you need to calculate the **average** value of all the numbers. To do this, add up all the measurements and then **divide by the number of measurements**.

Example: Let's say we measure the diameter of 5 pipes:

- Measurements: **20 mm, 22 mm, 21 mm, 19 mm, 22 mm.**

To find the average:

$$\text{Average (Mean)} = \frac{20 + 22 + 21 + 19 + 22}{5} = 20.8 \text{ mm}$$

Step 2: Subtract the Average from Each Measurement

Now, subtract the average from each measurement to see how far each number is from the average. These are called the **deviations**.

Example:

- 20 mm - 20.8 mm = -0.8 mm
- 22 mm - 20.8 mm = 1.2 mm
- 21 mm - 20.8 mm = 0.2 mm
- 19 mm - 20.8 mm = -1.8 mm
- 22 mm - 20.8 mm = 1.2 mm

Step 3: Square Each Deviation

To get rid of the negative values and make all the numbers **positive**, square each of these deviations (multiply each by itself).

Example:

- $(-0.8)^2 = 0.64$
- $(1.2)^2 = 1.44$
- $(0.2)^2 = 0.04$
- $(-1.8)^2 = 3.24$
- $(1.2)^2 = 1.44$

Step 4: Find the Average of These Squared Numbers

Add all the squared numbers together and **divide by the number of measurements**. This gives you the **variance**.

Example:

$$\text{Variance} = \frac{0.64 + 1.44 + 0.04 + 3.24 + 1.44}{5} = 1.36$$

Step 5: Take the Square Root

Finally, take the **square root** of the variance to get the **standard deviation**. This brings the value back to the original units.

Example:

$$\text{Standard Deviation} = \sqrt{1.36} \approx 1.17 \text{ mm}$$

Summary in Simple Terms

- **Average**: Find the middle value of all your data.
- **Deviation**: See how far each value is from the average.

- **Square the Differences**: Make sure all differences are positive by squaring them.
- **Find the Average of Those Squared Values**: This is called the **variance**.
- **Square Root the Variance**: This gives you the **standard deviation**, which tells you how spread out your data is.

What Does Standard Deviation Tell You?

- **Low Standard Deviation (e.g., 1.17 mm)**: The measurements are close to the average, meaning your process is **consistent**. The pipes produced are nearly all the same size.
- **High Standard Deviation (e.g., 3 or 4 mm)**: The measurements are very different from one another, indicating that the process is **inconsistent**, which can lead to **defective products** or **high scrap rates**.

In manufacturing, knowing the **standard deviation** helps determine if the process is in control or if it needs adjustments to reduce variability and improve quality.

Importance of Standard Deviation in Manufacturing

In manufacturing, **variability** is the enemy of quality. Too much variability can lead to defects, waste, and inconsistent products. **Standard deviation** helps manufacturers monitor **process variability** and make informed decisions about whether a process is **in control** or needs adjustments.

Common Uses of Standard Deviation in Manufacturing:

1. **Monitoring Product Quality**: Ensuring that products (e.g., pipe dimensions) consistently meet specifications.
2. **Process Control**: Keeping key process parameters (e.g., temperature, pressure) within acceptable limits.
3. **Reducing Defects**: Identifying and addressing sources of variability that lead to defects and waste.

Applying Standard Deviation to the Extruder Line Problem

The factory has noticed a **high scrap rate** (12%) on the **extruder lines** due to defects such as **brittleness** and **uneven wall thickness**. The team suspects that **temperature variability** during the extrusion process is contributing to these defects. To better understand the relationship between **temperature fluctuations** and **defects**, they will use **standard deviation** to quantify the variability in the extrusion process.

Step 1: Measuring Process Variability

The first step in applying standard deviation to the extruder line problem is to **collect data** on the key process variable—**temperature**. The team collects data from temperature sensors placed on extruder lines 1 and 2.

Data Collection:

- **Temperature readings** are taken every hour over a 2-week period.

- Data is recorded at various points in the extrusion process, including the **extruder barrel, die,** and **cooling sections**.
- For each batch of pipes, the team also records whether defects such as **brittleness** or **uneven thickness** occur.

Step 2: Calculating the Standard Deviation of Temperature Data

Once the data is collected, the team calculates the **mean temperature** and **standard deviation** to determine how much the temperature fluctuates from the average during the extrusion process.

Example Temperature Data (Extruder Line 1):

Time	Temperature (°C)
8:00 AM	215
9:00 AM	225
10:00 AM	230
11:00 AM	220
12:00 PM	235
1:00 PM	240
2:00 PM	220
3:00 PM	230

Calculating Mean:

$$\mu = \frac{215 + 225 + 230 + 220 + 235 + 240 + 220 + 230}{8} = 226.88°C$$

Calculating Standard Deviation:

Using the formula for standard deviation, the team calculates how much each temperature reading deviates from the mean and then squares the differences to calculate the overall standard deviation.

Standard Deviation Calculation Example:

1. Subtract the mean (226.88) from each temperature reading.
2. Square the result.
3. Find the average of the squared differences.
4. Take the square root of the result.

$$\sigma = \sqrt{\frac{1}{8}[(215 - 226.88)^2 + (225 - 226.88)^2 + \ldots + (230 - 226.88)^2]} = 8.18\,°C$$

Interpretation: The standard deviation of **8.18°C** indicates that there is a significant fluctuation in temperature around the mean (226.88°C). This variability could be causing the defects (e.g., brittleness), especially if the temperature exceeds optimal levels for polyethylene extrusion.

Step 3: Analyzing the Impact of Temperature Variability on Defects

With the standard deviation calculated, the team now examines how the temperature fluctuations correlate with the **defects** observed on the extruder lines.

Defects and Temperature Variability:

- The team observes that when the **temperature exceeds 230°C**, the pipes are more likely to become **brittle**.
- When the temperature fluctuates more than ±5°C from the mean, **uneven thickness** defects become more frequent.

- The **standard deviation of 8.18°C** is too high for consistent pipe quality—indicating that the process is not under control and requires adjustments.

Step 4: Using Control Charts to Monitor Standard Deviation

To continuously monitor the **temperature variability** and keep it under control, the team sets up **Control Charts** that track the **mean temperature** and **standard deviation** over time. Control charts help identify when the process is drifting out of control, signaling the need for corrective action.

Control Chart Components:

1. **Centerline (CL)**: The mean temperature (226.88°C).
2. **Upper Control Limit (UCL)**: The highest acceptable temperature before defects occur (e.g., 230°C).
3. **Lower Control Limit (LCL)**: The lowest acceptable temperature (e.g., 220°C).
4. **Standard Deviation Line**: Tracks temperature variability over time.

Example Control Chart:

Time	Temperature (°C)	Standard Deviation
8:00 AM	215	8.18°C
9:00 AM	225	7.50°C
10:00 AM	230	6.90°C
11:00 AM	220	6.80°C

If the **standard deviation** starts to exceed acceptable limits, the team will investigate the cause (e.g., equipment malfunction, material inconsistencies) and take corrective action to stabilize the process.

Step 5: Reducing Standard Deviation to Improve Quality

After identifying that **temperature variability** is the primary cause of defects, the team works to **reduce the standard deviation** and bring the process under control. By lowering the standard deviation, they can ensure that the temperature stays within a tight range, reducing defects such as **brittleness** and **uneven thickness**.

Methods to Reduce Standard Deviation:

1. **Upgrade Temperature Control System**: Install a more precise temperature control system that can maintain consistent temperatures within ±2°C of the target.
2. **Implement Preventive Maintenance**: Regularly calibrate the temperature control system to prevent temperature drift.
3. **Train Operators**: Train operators to monitor temperature fluctuations and make adjustments before the temperature moves out of control.
4. **Use Poka-Yoke**: Implement mistake-proofing mechanisms (e.g., sensors that shut down the extruder if the temperature exceeds limits) to prevent overheating.

By reducing the **standard deviation** from **8.18°C to 3°C**, the team can significantly reduce the scrap rate and ensure more consistent product quality.

Step 6: Monitoring Ongoing Variability with SPC

To sustain the improvements, the team will use **Statistical Process Control (SPC)** methods, including continuous use of **control charts** and monitoring of **standard deviation**. This will allow them to quickly detect any drift in process parameters and take corrective actions before defects occur.

- **Example Ongoing Monitoring**: The team sets a target standard deviation of **3°C**. If the standard deviation rises above this limit, the system will trigger an alarm, prompting an operator to investigate and correct the issue.

Conclusion: Understanding and Managing Process Variability with Standard Deviation

In this chapter, we explored how **standard deviation** is used to understand and manage **process variability** in a manufacturing setting. By calculating the standard deviation of temperature data on the extruder lines, the team was able to quantify the level of variability and correlate it with defects such as **brittleness** and **uneven wall thickness**.

Through process adjustments, such as installing a more precise temperature control system and implementing **preventive maintenance** procedures, the team was able to reduce the **standard deviation** and stabilize the process. This led to a significant reduction in the **scrap rate**, improved consistency, and higher-quality products.

Standard deviation is a critical tool for identifying, analyzing, and controlling **process variability**. When used alongside tools like **control charts** and **SPC**, it enables manufacturers to maintain high standards of quality and minimize waste, ensuring their processes are efficient and reliable over time.

Here's a step-by-step explanation of how you can create an Excel formula to calculate **standard deviation**:

Step-by-Step Guide to Writing an Excel Formula for Standard Deviation

1. **Input Your Data**:
   - Enter your data points into a column in Excel. For example:
     - **A1**: 20
     - **A2**: 22
     - **A3**: 21
     - **A4**: 19
     - **A5**: 22
2. **Use the Built-In Function for Standard Deviation**:
   - Excel provides several built-in functions for calculating standard deviation. The most commonly used one for sample data is STDEV.S( ), and for population data, it is STDEV.P( ).
   - For our purposes, let's assume we want to calculate the standard deviation for the population, so we'll use STDEV.P( ).
   - In an empty cell, type the formula:

=STDEV.P(A1:A5)

   - Press **Enter**, and Excel will calculate the standard deviation for you.

Explanation of the Formula

- **STDEV.P(range)**: This calculates the **standard deviation** for the entire population, which means all of the data points in the dataset are taken into account.
- **STDEV.S(range)**: This calculates the **standard deviation for a sample** if you are only looking at a subset of the total data.

Manual Calculation Using Excel Formulas

If you want to calculate each part manually (using Excel functions to perform each calculation step), follow these steps:

1. **Calculate the Mean (Average)**:
   - In an empty cell (e.g., **B1**), enter:

   =AVERAGE(A1:A5)

   - This will give you the **mean** of the data points.
2. **Calculate Each Deviation from the Mean**:
   - In cells **B2** to **B6**, calculate the deviation of each data point from the mean. Enter the following formula in **B2**:

   =A2 - B1

   - Drag the formula down to **B6** to calculate deviations for each value. The **B1** keeps the mean fixed as you drag the formula.

3. **Square Each Deviation**:
    - In cells **C2** to **C6**, enter the formula to calculate the **squared deviations**:

    =B2^2

    - Drag this formula down to **C6** to square each deviation.
4. **Calculate the Average of Squared Deviations (Variance)**:
    - In an empty cell (e.g., **D1**), enter:

    =AVERAGE(C2:C6)

    - This will give you the **variance**.
5. **Take the Square Root of the Variance (Standard Deviation)**:
    - In an empty cell (e.g., **E1**), enter:

    =SQRT(D1)

    - This will give you the **standard deviation**.

Summary of Using Excel

- **Quick Method**: Use =STDEV.P(A1:A5) or =STDEV.S(A1:A5) to calculate the standard deviation directly.
- **Manual Method**: You can use a combination of AVERAGE( ), subtraction, squaring (^2), AVERAGE( ), and SQRT( ) to calculate the standard deviation step by step.

The **quick method** using STDEV.P or STDEV.S is generally the most efficient way to find the standard deviation in Excel, as it allows you to avoid manual calculations and the potential for errors.

Chapter 6: Poka-Yoke – Error-Proofing for Process Reliability

Introduction to Poka-Yoke

Poka-Yoke (pronounced poh-kah yoh-keh) is a **Lean manufacturing tool** designed to prevent errors by **"mistake-proofing"** processes. The term, coined by **Shigeo Shingo**, a leading figure in the development of the **Toyota Production System**, means **"to avoid mistakes"** in Japanese. The goal of Poka-Yoke is to design processes and systems in such a way that **errors become impossible** or are **immediately detected and corrected** before they result in defects.

In manufacturing, **defects** and **waste** often arise from human error or equipment malfunctions. By using Poka-Yoke, these mistakes can be prevented or minimized. This chapter will explore how **Poka-Yoke** can be applied to **error-proof** the extrusion process in a **polyethylene pipe manufacturing factory** that is experiencing a **high scrap rate**. Specifically, we will show how Poka-Yoke can be used to address the root cause of the high scrap rate—**fluctuating temperatures** on the extruder lines.

Why Poka-Yoke is Important in Manufacturing

In manufacturing environments, even small mistakes can lead to **defects**, **wasted materials**, and **increased**

costs. By integrating Poka-Yoke techniques, manufacturers can:

- **Eliminate errors** before they occur or catch them early.
- **Ensure consistency** in processes and product quality.
- **Reduce defects** and scrap, leading to lower costs and increased efficiency.
- **Enhance safety** by preventing human mistakes that could cause accidents.

Poka-Yoke systems are typically **simple** and **inexpensive** to implement. They can take the form of physical devices, automatic shutdowns, warning signals, or even visual cues that guide operators toward error-free work.

Types of Poka-Yoke

There are two main categories of Poka-Yoke:

1. **Prevention Poka-Yoke**: This stops errors from occurring in the first place.
   - Example: A machine won't start unless all parts are correctly positioned.
2. **Detection Poka-Yoke**: This detects errors before they lead to defects and signals operators to take corrective action.
   - Example: A sensor alerts the operator if temperatures exceed a safe threshold.

Applying Poka-Yoke to the Extruder Line Problem

In our **polyethylene pipe manufacturing factory**, the issue of **high scrap rates** has been traced back to

fluctuating temperatures on the extruder lines. Excessive or inconsistent temperatures during extrusion lead to defects like **brittleness** and **uneven wall thickness**, which result in **scrapped products**.

Poka-Yoke will be used to **error-proof the temperature control system** and ensure that temperatures remain within the desired range to prevent these defects from occurring.

Step 1: Identifying the Root Cause of Errors

Before applying Poka-Yoke, the first step is to clearly identify the **root cause** of the errors that are leading to defects. In this case, the **DMAIC process** revealed that the high scrap rate was caused by **overheating** during the extrusion process, which was a result of a **malfunctioning temperature control system**.

- **Problem Statement**: Temperature fluctuations on the extruder lines are causing polyethylene pipes to be defective, particularly resulting in **brittleness** when temperatures exceed 230°C.
- **Goal**: Prevent temperature fluctuations from occurring and ensure that the extruder operates within the specified temperature range.

Common Errors Leading to Defects:

1. **Overheating of the material** due to malfunctioning or uncalibrated temperature control systems.
2. **Manual adjustments by operators** that lead to incorrect temperature settings.
3. **Delayed response to temperature spikes**, causing defects before corrective action is taken.

Step 2: Designing Poka-Yoke Solutions

Once the errors are identified, the next step is to design **Poka-Yoke mechanisms** to prevent or detect these errors. The focus is on ensuring that **temperature control errors** are minimized or caught early.

1. Prevention Poka-Yoke: Automating the Temperature Control System

One of the primary errors identified is that operators occasionally **manually adjust the temperature settings**, resulting in incorrect or fluctuating temperatures. A **Prevention Poka-Yoke** solution would involve **automating the temperature control system** to eliminate the need for manual adjustments.

Solution:

- **Install an automated temperature control system** that automatically maintains the correct temperature throughout the extrusion process.
- **Eliminate manual temperature adjustments** by locking operator access to temperature settings during production.
- Use **pre-set temperature ranges** based on material specifications to ensure consistency in production.

Benefits:

- Prevents human error in adjusting temperature settings.
- Ensures the temperature remains within the specified range, reducing the likelihood of defects caused by overheating.

2. Detection Poka-Yoke: Temperature Sensors with Automatic Shutdown

Even with an automated system, there is still the possibility that equipment could malfunction. In this case, a **Detection Poka-Yoke** solution can be implemented to catch any temperature deviations and prevent defective pipes from being produced.

Solution:

- **Install temperature sensors** on the extruder lines that continuously monitor the temperature.
- Program the system to **automatically shut down** the extruder if the temperature exceeds a safe limit (e.g., 230°C).
- Use **visual alarms** or **audio alerts** to notify operators when the temperature is approaching unsafe levels, giving them time to take corrective action.

Benefits:

- Catches temperature deviations before they cause defects.
- Reduces the chance of producing defective pipes due to undetected overheating.
- Improves safety by automatically shutting down equipment if overheating occurs.

3. Visual Poka-Yoke: Color-Coded Temperature Indicators

Another simple yet effective Poka-Yoke solution is to use **visual aids** to help operators monitor temperature conditions in real-time.

Solution:

- **Install color-coded temperature indicators** on the control panel of the extruder:
  - **Green**: Temperature is within the safe operating range (e.g., 220°C–230°C).
  - **Yellow**: Temperature is approaching the upper or lower limit (e.g., above 230°C or below 220°C).
  - **Red**: Temperature has exceeded the acceptable limit, and immediate corrective action is needed.
- Use **LED displays** or **digital screens** that provide clear visual feedback to operators, making it easy to identify when corrective action is needed.

Benefits:

- Allows operators to quickly and easily see if the process is within acceptable limits.
- Reduces response time to deviations, minimizing the chance of defects.
- Simple and inexpensive to implement.

4. Error-Proofing Maintenance: Preventive Maintenance Poka-Yoke

In addition to controlling temperatures during production, it's crucial to ensure that the **temperature control system is maintained** properly. An effective Poka-Yoke solution would be to implement **preventive maintenance** schedules that reduce the likelihood of system malfunctions.

Solution:

- Set up **automatic reminders** or **calibration schedules** for the temperature control system, ensuring it is regularly maintained and checked.

- Use **Poka-Yoke software** that disables the extruder if a scheduled maintenance or calibration is missed.

Benefits:

- Ensures the temperature control system is regularly calibrated, reducing the chance of future malfunctions.
- Proactively prevents defects that result from an uncalibrated or faulty temperature control system.

Step 3: Implementing and Testing Poka-Yoke Solutions

Once the Poka-Yoke mechanisms have been designed, the next step is to **implement** them on the extruder lines and **test** their effectiveness.

Implementation Plan:

1. **Install Automated Temperature Control System**: Set up the automated system on extruder lines 1 and 2, with pre-programmed temperature ranges.
2. **Install Temperature Sensors and Automatic Shutdown**: Equip the extruder lines with temperature sensors that automatically shut down the system if temperatures exceed the set limits.
3. **Set Up Visual Indicators**: Install color-coded displays on the control panel that alert operators to temperature conditions.
4. **Schedule Preventive Maintenance**: Program automatic reminders for system calibration and integrate a lock-out system if maintenance is missed.

Step 4: Monitoring and Adjusting Poka-Yoke Solutions

After implementing Poka-Yoke, the team needs to **monitor the effectiveness** of the solutions and adjust them if necessary. The goal is to continuously **improve the process** and ensure that errors are consistently prevented or caught early.

1. Monitor Key Metrics:

- **Scrap Rate**: Track the scrap rate over time to ensure that it decreases as a result of the Poka-Yoke solutions.
- **Temperature Stability**: Monitor temperature data to ensure the automated system is maintaining stable temperatures within the desired range.
- **Downtime**: Measure any downtime caused by automatic shutdowns and investigate the reasons behind temperature spikes.

2. Continuous Improvement:

- **Refine Visual Indicators**: If operators report difficulties in interpreting the color-coded indicators, make adjustments to improve clarity.
- **Improve Training**: Ensure that all operators are trained to understand how the Poka-Yoke systems work and how to respond to any alerts or shutdowns.

Conclusion: The Power of Poka-Yoke for Error-Proofing

Poka-Yoke is a powerful tool for **eliminating errors** and **improving consistency** in manufacturing processes. By applying Poka-Yoke to the **temperature control system** on the extruder lines, the **polyethylene**

pipe manufacturing factory was able to **error-proof** the process, reducing temperature fluctuations that led to defects.

The combination of **automated controls, sensor-based shutdowns,** and **visual indicators** ensured that **human error** and **equipment malfunctions** were minimized. This resulted in a significant reduction in the **scrap rate**, improved product quality, and a more stable manufacturing process.

Poka-Yoke techniques are flexible and can be applied to various manufacturing challenges, making them an essential part of any **continuous improvement** or **Lean manufacturing** strategy. By designing processes that prevent mistakes or catch them before they lead to defects, companies can achieve **higher quality, lower costs**, and **greater efficiency**.

Chapter 7: D.O.W.N.T.I.M.E. – The 8 Common Forms of Waste in Lean Manufacturing

Introduction to D.O.W.N.T.I.M.E.

In Lean Manufacturing, **waste** is any activity that consumes resources but does not add value to the customer. Reducing waste is critical for improving efficiency, cutting costs, and ensuring that processes are streamlined. One of the foundational concepts of Lean is understanding the **8 common types of waste**, collectively referred to by the acronym **D.O.W.N.T.I.M.E.**

This chapter will explore the **8 forms of waste** and how they can be identified and eliminated in the context of a **polyethylene pipe manufacturing factory**, focusing on the extruder lines where **high scrap rates** have been observed. By applying the principles of D.O.W.N.T.I.M.E., the team will uncover areas of waste contributing to inefficiencies and propose solutions to **eliminate waste**, improve process efficiency, and reduce the overall scrap rate.

What is D.O.W.N.T.I.M.E.?

The acronym **D.O.W.N.T.I.M.E.** stands for the **8 types of waste** commonly found in manufacturing environments:

1. **Defects**
2. **Overproduction**
3. **Waiting**
4. **Non-Utilized Talent**

5. Transportation
6. Inventory
7. Motion
8. Extra Processing

Each form of waste reduces efficiency and adds cost without adding value to the customer. In the case of the **extruder lines** in the factory, addressing these wastes can lead to significant improvements in **process flow**, **material use**, and **overall production efficiency**.

D: Defects – Waste from Producing Defective Products

Defects are one of the most obvious forms of waste. Any product that doesn't meet specifications, requires rework, or is scrapped outright adds cost without delivering value. In our example, the factory is producing polyethylene pipes with defects such as **brittleness** and **uneven wall thickness** due to temperature control issues.

Identifying Defects on the Extruder Lines:

- **Current Scrap Rate**: The factory is scrapping **12%** of the pipes produced on extruder lines 1 and 2 due to defects.
- **Common Defects**: These include **brittleness** (due to overheating) and **uneven thickness** (due to inconsistent temperature control).

Solutions to Reduce Defects:

- **Poka-Yoke** systems (error-proofing): Implement temperature sensors and automated shutdowns to prevent overheating.

- **Standard Operating Procedures (SOPs)**: Create and enforce SOPs for setting and maintaining optimal temperature ranges.

By reducing defects, the factory can reduce material waste, lower costs, and increase overall efficiency.

O: Overproduction – Waste from Producing More Than Needed

Overproduction occurs when a company produces more than is required by demand. This leads to excess inventory, wasted resources, and higher costs. In Lean, overproduction is considered one of the most significant wastes because it triggers other types of waste, such as excess inventory and unnecessary transportation.

Identifying Overproduction on the Extruder Lines:

- **Current Situation**: The factory produces pipes in large batches, often exceeding customer demand. Some batches are scrapped due to defects, but even non-defective pipes sit in inventory awaiting future orders.

Solutions to Reduce Overproduction:

- **Just-in-Time (JIT) Production**: Implement JIT principles, producing only the quantity needed to meet customer demand.
- **Demand Forecasting**: Improve demand forecasting to align production with customer needs, reducing excess production.

Reducing overproduction ensures that the factory is only producing what is needed, preventing the accumulation of unnecessary inventory and wasted materials.

W: Waiting – Waste from Idle Time

Waiting refers to any downtime where workers, machines, or materials are idle. This can happen due to bottlenecks in the process, unplanned maintenance, or inefficient scheduling. In our example, the extruder lines may experience waiting due to **machine downtime** or **die changes** that take longer than expected.

Identifying Waiting on the Extruder Lines:

- **Current Situation**: Frequent die changes on the extruder lines cause significant downtime, as operators wait for the machines to be ready for the next batch. Inconsistent temperatures also lead to delays as operators wait for the system to stabilize.

Solutions to Reduce Waiting:

- **SMED (Single-Minute Exchange of Dies)**: Implement SMED techniques to reduce the time taken to change dies, minimizing machine downtime.
- **Preventive Maintenance**: Schedule regular maintenance to reduce unplanned downtime and ensure that equipment is operating smoothly.
- **Process Flow Optimization**: Analyze the production workflow to reduce bottlenecks and improve machine availability.

Reducing waiting times helps increase machine utilization, reduces bottlenecks, and improves overall production efficiency.

N: Non-Utilized Talent – Waste from Underutilizing Skills

Non-Utilized Talent refers to not using employees' skills, knowledge, or creativity to their full potential. This waste occurs when workers are performing tasks below their skill level or when their suggestions for improvement are not heard or implemented.

Identifying Non-Utilized Talent on the Extruder Lines:

- **Current Situation**: Operators on the extruder lines are highly skilled but are spending a lot of time making manual adjustments to the temperature control system or performing routine tasks that could be automated. They are not being involved in process improvement discussions.

Solutions to Address Non-Utilized Talent:

- **Employee Training**: Train operators to take on more responsibility, such as managing the automated temperature control system and identifying areas for continuous improvement.
- **Employee Engagement Programs**: Create channels for operators to provide feedback and suggestions for process improvements, ensuring their expertise is utilized in decision-making.
- **Automation of Routine Tasks**: Automate tasks such as temperature adjustments to free up operators for higher-value work, such as quality control and process monitoring.

By engaging employees and using their full potential, the factory can improve innovation, efficiency, and employee satisfaction.

T: Transportation – Waste from Unnecessary Movement of Materials

Transportation waste occurs when materials are moved unnecessarily between workstations, machines, or storage areas. Excess transportation increases lead times and introduces opportunities for damage or loss of materials.

Identifying Transportation Waste on the Extruder Lines:

- **Current Situation**: Raw polyethylene pellets are transported from storage to the extruder lines in large batches, often requiring multiple trips back and forth between the warehouse and the production floor. Finished pipes are also moved between workstations inefficiently.

Solutions to Reduce Transportation Waste:

- **Reorganize the Production Layout**: Design a more efficient factory layout where materials and products flow smoothly through the production process with minimal movement.
- **Just-in-Time Material Delivery**: Implement JIT systems for delivering materials to the extruder lines only when needed, reducing the need for excess transportation and material handling.

Reducing transportation waste can significantly streamline operations and reduce unnecessary movement of materials, leading to faster production times.

I: Inventory – Waste from Excess Inventory

Inventory waste occurs when there is more raw material, work-in-progress, or finished goods than is necessary to meet current demand. Excess inventory ties up capital, takes up valuable space, and increases the risk of product damage or obsolescence.

Identifying Inventory Waste on the Extruder Lines:

- **Current Situation**: The factory keeps large quantities of raw polyethylene pellets and finished pipes in storage. Because production sometimes exceeds demand, finished products can sit in inventory for weeks before being shipped to customers.

Solutions to Reduce Inventory Waste:

- **Kanban System**: Implement a **Kanban** system to manage inventory levels and ensure that materials are only replenished when they are used.
- **Align Production with Demand**: Use demand forecasting to better align production schedules with customer orders, reducing the need for excess inventory.

By reducing inventory, the factory can free up storage space, reduce the risk of damage, and lower costs associated with storing and managing excess materials.

M: Motion – Waste from Unnecessary Movements by Workers

Motion waste occurs when workers move more than necessary to complete tasks. This could involve reaching for tools, walking long distances to access materials, or performing repetitive motions that could be streamlined or automated.

Identifying Motion Waste on the Extruder Lines:

- **Current Situation**: Operators frequently move between different sections of the production floor to adjust machines, retrieve tools, or monitor temperatures. This adds to fatigue and reduces productivity.

Solutions to Reduce Motion Waste:

- **Workstation Design**: Reorganize workstations to minimize the need for excessive walking or reaching for tools. Ensure that tools, controls, and materials are within easy reach.
- **Automation**: Automate repetitive tasks such as temperature monitoring and adjustments to reduce unnecessary operator movement.
- **5S Methodology**: Implement the **5S** workplace organization system (Sort, Set in Order, Shine, Standardize, Sustain) to ensure a clean, organized, and efficient workspace.

Reducing unnecessary motion not only improves efficiency but also reduces worker fatigue and the risk of injury.

E: Extra Processing – Waste from Doing More Work Than Necessary

Extra processing refers to doing more work or using more resources than what is needed to meet customer requirements. This can involve unnecessary steps in the production process, redundant quality checks, or over-engineering products.

Identifying Extra Processing on the Extruder Lines:

- **Current Situation**: Operators perform multiple quality checks on the finished pipes, even when defects are rare, leading to redundant inspections. Additionally, some pipes are reworked multiple times due to inconsistent specifications.

Solutions to Reduce Extra Processing Waste:

- **Simplify Quality Control**: Use automated quality control systems to ensure that checks are performed only when necessary and defects are caught early in the process, eliminating redundant inspections.
- **Process Optimization**: Streamline the extrusion process to ensure pipes are produced to the correct specifications the first time, reducing the need for rework.

Reducing extra processing ensures that the factory is only doing what is necessary to deliver high-quality products, saving time and resources.

Conclusion: Eliminating Waste with D.O.W.N.T.I.M.E.

By understanding and addressing the **8 common forms of waste** represented by **D.O.W.N.T.I.M.E.**, the polyethylene pipe manufacturing factory can improve overall efficiency, reduce scrap, and lower costs. Each form of waste contributes to inefficiency and lost value, but by systematically identifying and eliminating them, the factory can streamline its operations and better meet customer demands.

From reducing **defects** and **overproduction** to minimizing **motion** and **extra processing**, focusing on eliminating waste creates a Leaner, more efficient process. By embedding these waste-reduction principles into daily operations, the factory can sustain long-term improvements, enhance product quality, and remain competitive in the marketplace.

D.O.W.N.T.I.M.E. is a fundamental concept in Lean manufacturing that drives **continuous improvement**, and when applied effectively, it enables organizations to achieve higher levels of productivity, quality, and customer satisfaction.

Chapter 8: Key Performance Indicators (KPIs) – Measuring and Managing Performance

Introduction to KPIs in Manufacturing

Key Performance Indicators (KPIs) are measurable values that demonstrate how effectively a company or process is achieving specific objectives. In the context of **manufacturing**, KPIs are essential for tracking operational performance, identifying areas for improvement, and ensuring that production goals align with the company's overall strategy.

KPIs help manufacturing teams measure critical aspects such as **production efficiency, quality, costs**, and **delivery timelines**. By regularly monitoring KPIs, factories can maintain **continuous improvement**, ensure **consistent product quality**, and achieve greater **operational efficiency**.

In this chapter, we will delve into **how to define, track, and use KPIs** in a **polyethylene pipe manufacturing factory**, particularly focusing on how KPIs can be leveraged to improve the **extruder line processes** that have been experiencing **high scrap rates** due to temperature fluctuations. KPIs will help the team understand **what is happening, why it is happening,** and **how to improve it.**

Why KPIs are Important

KPIs serve as a **quantitative gauge** of how well a process or department is performing. They enable manufacturers to:

- **Make data-driven decisions**: By providing clear, measurable outcomes, KPIs allow for informed decision-making based on real-time data.
- **Track progress toward goals**: KPIs help teams monitor how well they are progressing toward specific performance targets, such as reducing scrap or improving cycle times.
- **Identify problems early**: KPIs allow teams to detect issues like production inefficiencies, quality problems, or cost overruns before they escalate.
- **Benchmark performance**: KPIs allow comparison with industry standards or past performance, helping to identify areas where the factory is underperforming.

Types of KPIs in Manufacturing

KPIs can be categorized into different types based on the area of focus. Below are some of the most relevant KPIs in **manufacturing**:

1. **Efficiency KPIs**
   - **Overall Equipment Effectiveness (OEE)**
   - **Cycle Time**
   - **Capacity Utilization**
2. **Quality KPIs**
   - **Scrap Rate**
   - **First Pass Yield (FPY)**
   - **Defects per Million Opportunities (DPMO)**
3. **Cost KPIs**
   - **Cost per Unit**
   - **Labor Productivity**
   - **Material Usage Variance**
4. **Delivery KPIs**
   - **On-Time Delivery (OTD)**
   - **Lead Time**
   - **Order Cycle Time**

In the **polyethylene pipe manufacturing factory**, we will focus on KPIs that track performance on the **extruder lines**, including **scrap rate, cycle time**, and **OEE**, as well as KPIs that track the performance of the **temperature control system**, which was identified as the root cause of the defects.

Defining Effective KPIs for the Extruder Line Process

For KPIs to be effective, they must be **clear, measurable, relevant**, and **actionable**. When defining KPIs for the extruder lines in our factory, we should follow the **SMART criteria**:

- **Specific**: KPIs should be well-defined and target a specific area.
- **Measurable**: KPIs must be quantifiable so that progress can be tracked.
- **Achievable**: Targets should be realistic based on current resources.
- **Relevant**: KPIs must be aligned with business objectives.
- **Time-Bound**: KPIs should have a defined time frame for achieving targets.

Example KPIs for the Extruder Lines:

1. **Scrap Rate**: The percentage of polyethylene pipes that are scrapped due to defects.
   - **Target**: Reduce the scrap rate from **12%** to **2%** within 6 months.
2. **Cycle Time**: The average time it takes to complete the extrusion of one pipe.
   - **Target**: Reduce the cycle time from **10 minutes** per pipe to **8 minutes** within 3 months.

3. **Overall Equipment Effectiveness (OEE)**: A measure of how well the extruder lines are performing based on **availability, performance**, and **quality**.
   - **Target**: Increase OEE from **70%** to **85%** by minimizing downtime and improving throughput.
4. **First Pass Yield (FPY)**: The percentage of pipes that are manufactured correctly without the need for rework or repair.
   - **Target**: Improve FPY from **85%** to **95%** within 4 months by addressing temperature fluctuations that cause defects.
5. **Temperature Stability**: The percentage of time the temperature control system operates within the optimal range.
   - **Target**: Ensure the system operates within **±5°C** of the target temperature for **98%** of the production time.

Key Manufacturing KPIs Explained

1. Scrap Rate:

The **scrap rate** is one of the most critical KPIs for our factory. It measures the percentage of defective pipes produced that must be discarded or reworked.

Formula:

$$\text{Scrap Rate} = \frac{\text{Number of Defective Products}}{\text{Total Number of Products Produced}} \times 100$$

Example: If the factory produces 10,000 pipes in a month and 1,200 are scrapped due to defects, the scrap rate is:

$$\frac{1200}{10000} \times 100 = 12\%$$

Actionable Insights: Monitoring the scrap rate allows the team to evaluate the impact of the **temperature control system** on product quality. A decreasing scrap rate signals that improvements are working, while an increasing scrap rate would prompt further investigation.

2. Overall Equipment Effectiveness (OEE):

OEE is a **comprehensive KPI** that measures how effectively production equipment is being used. It breaks down into three factors:

- **Availability**: The percentage of scheduled production time that the equipment is available to operate.
- **Performance**: How well the equipment performs relative to its maximum potential.
- **Quality**: The percentage of good products produced compared to total products.
- **Formula**:

$$OEE = \text{Availability} \times \text{Performance} \times \text{Quality}$$

Example: If the extruder line is available **90%** of the time, runs at **80%** of its ideal speed, and produces **95%** good quality pipes, the OEE would be:

$$OEE = 0.90 \times 0.80 \times 0.95 = 0.684 \text{ or } 68.4\%$$

Actionable Insights: A low OEE could indicate excessive downtime, slow cycle times, or high defect rates. By monitoring OEE, the team can identify **bottlenecks** in the extrusion process and make improvements in specific areas.

3. Cycle Time:

The **cycle time** measures how long it takes to complete one cycle of production, from start to finish. In this case, it refers to the time it takes to extrude and finish one polyethylene pipe.

- **Formula**:

$$\text{Cycle Time} = \frac{\text{Total Production Time}}{\text{Number of Products Produced}}$$

Example: If the extruder line operates for 500 minutes in a day and produces 50 pipes, the cycle time is:

$$\frac{500}{50} = 10 \text{ minutes per pipe}$$

- **Actionable Insights**: Reducing the cycle time means increasing the efficiency of the extrusion process. By analyzing cycle time, the factory can look for ways to eliminate **bottlenecks** and **reduce downtime** between cycles.

4. First Pass Yield (FPY):

FPY measures the percentage of products that are manufactured correctly the first time without needing rework or repair. It is a strong indicator of **process quality** and **consistency**.

Formula:

$$FPY = \frac{\text{Number of Good Products Produced}}{\text{Total Number of Products Produced}} \times 100$$

Example: If the factory produces 1,000 pipes and 950 are defect-free on the first pass, the FPY is:

$$\frac{950}{1000} \times 100 = 95\%$$

- **Actionable Insights**: FPY is an important metric for ensuring that processes are producing high-quality products. An increase in FPY shows that fewer defects are occurring, while a decrease indicates that the root cause of defects needs to be addressed.

5. Temperature Stability:

For the extruder line, **temperature stability** is crucial in producing high-quality pipes. This KPI measures how often the temperature stays within the optimal range during production.

Formula:

$$\text{Temperature Stability} = \frac{\text{Time Within Target Range}}{\text{Total Production Time}} \times 100$$

- **Example**: If the temperature control system is within the acceptable range for 98 out of 100 hours of production time, the stability rate is:

$$\frac{98}{100} \times 100 = 98\%$$

Actionable Insights: Monitoring temperature stability helps the team ensure that the **root cause** of the scrap (temperature fluctuations) is being controlled. A high temperature stability indicates that the process is under control, while fluctuations would signal the need for corrective action.

Using KPIs for Continuous Improvement

KPIs are not just tools for **monitoring performance**—they are also critical for **driving continuous improvement**. Here's how KPIs are used to enhance manufacturing processes:

1. Regular Performance Reviews:

Schedule **weekly** or **monthly reviews** of KPI data to assess whether the factory is meeting its targets. This provides an opportunity to catch issues early and adjust strategies as necessary.

2. Root Cause Analysis:

When KPIs indicate that performance is below target (e.g., scrap rate increases or OEE drops), use **root cause analysis** tools like the **5 Whys** or **Fishbone Diagrams** to investigate why the issue is happening and implement corrective actions.

3. Benchmarking and Goal Setting:

Use KPI data to benchmark performance against **industry standards** or past performance. Set realistic, time-bound goals for improving each KPI, and continuously raise the bar as targets are achieved.

4. Employee Involvement:

Involve employees at all levels in KPI tracking and analysis. Operators, engineers, and management should be aware of the KPIs relevant to their roles and work collaboratively to meet targets.

5. Data-Driven Decisions:

Use KPIs to make informed, data-driven decisions about where to focus improvement efforts. For example, if OEE is low due to downtime, focus on preventive maintenance and process optimization to improve availability and performance.

Conclusion: The Role of KPIs in Manufacturing Excellence

Key Performance Indicators (KPIs) are vital for measuring, managing, and improving the performance of manufacturing processes. By tracking relevant KPIs such as **scrap rate, cycle time, OEE**, and **temperature stability**, the **polyethylene pipe manufacturing factory** can continuously monitor the health of the **extruder line** processes, identify issues early, and make **data-driven improvements**.

Effective use of KPIs enables manufacturers to:

- **Increase efficiency** by identifying bottlenecks and reducing waste.
- **Improve product quality** by monitoring defect rates and process consistency.
- **Reduce costs** by optimizing resource usage and reducing scrap.
- **Enhance decision-making** by providing clear insights into operational performance.

KPIs provide a **feedback loop** for continuous improvement, helping teams stay focused on their goals, ensure alignment with business objectives, and maintain a culture of **operational excellence**.

Chapter 9: The 5 Whys – A Simple and Effective Root Cause Analysis Tool

Introduction to the 5 Whys

The **5 Whys** is a simple yet powerful tool used to perform **root cause analysis** in problem-solving processes. By repeatedly asking the question "**Why?**," this technique helps you drill down to the **root cause** of a problem rather than focusing on surface-level symptoms. The **5 Whys method** is often employed as part of Lean and Six Sigma methodologies to identify and eliminate issues at their source, preventing them from recurring.

The 5 Whys technique was popularized by **Sakichi Toyoda**, the founder of Toyota, and it has since become a cornerstone of the **Toyota Production System** and **Lean Manufacturing**. The method encourages teams to avoid jumping to conclusions or implementing superficial fixes. Instead, it promotes deeper thinking to uncover the underlying causes of issues.

In this chapter, we will explain how the **5 Whys process** works and apply it to a real-world example in a **polyethylene pipe manufacturing factory**, where the team uses it to investigate and solve the problem of **high scrap rates** on the extruder lines.

What is the 5 Whys Process?

The **5 Whys** technique is a structured approach for identifying the root cause of a problem by asking "Why?" multiple times—usually five, but sometimes more or fewer depending on the complexity of the problem. Each answer leads to the next "Why" question, allowing you to peel back layers of symptoms until the fundamental issue is uncovered.

Key Characteristics of the 5 Whys:

- **Simple and intuitive**: The process doesn't require advanced statistical tools or extensive training, making it accessible to all team members.
- **Collaborative**: It fosters teamwork by encouraging cross-functional discussion and input.
- **Focuses on root causes**: By going beyond symptoms, the 5 Whys help identify the real source of the issue, leading to more effective solutions.

The 5 Whys Process: Step-by-Step

To effectively use the 5 Whys, follow these steps:

1. Define the Problem

Start by clearly identifying the problem you want to investigate. This should be a specific, measurable issue. In our example, the problem is the **high scrap rate** on the extruder lines, which is leading to significant material waste and increased costs.

- **Example Problem Statement**: The scrap rate on extruder lines 1 and 2 has reached **12%**, which is well above the acceptable level of 2%. Most defects are caused by **brittleness** and **uneven wall thickness** in the pipes.

2. Ask the First "Why?"

Ask why the problem is happening. The first "Why" question should target the most obvious symptom of the problem.

- **First Why**: Why is the scrap rate on extruder lines 1 and 2 so high?
  - **Answer**: Because many of the pipes are brittle and have uneven thickness.

3. Ask the Second "Why?"

After getting the answer to the first question, ask "Why" again to explore the underlying cause of the issue described in the previous answer.

- **Second Why**: Why are the pipes brittle and uneven in thickness?
  - **Answer**: Because the **temperature on the extruder lines** is inconsistent and often too high during the extrusion process.

4. Ask the Third "Why?"

Repeat the process. The third "Why" should further narrow down the cause, moving closer to the root issue.

- **Third Why**: Why is the temperature on the extruder lines inconsistent and too high?
  - **Answer**: Because the **temperature control system** on the extruder lines is malfunctioning, and operators are adjusting the temperature manually.

5. Ask the Fourth "Why?"

Keep digging deeper. Each level of questioning should help clarify the cause-and-effect relationship leading to the issue.

- **Fourth Why**: Why is the temperature control system malfunctioning, requiring manual adjustments?
  - **Answer**: Because the system hasn't been **calibrated** or properly maintained in over a year.

6. Ask the Fifth "Why?"

Finally, ask "Why" one more time to identify the root cause. At this stage, the problem should be defined in its entirety, and the solution will likely address this root cause.

- **Fifth Why**: Why hasn't the temperature control system been calibrated or maintained?
  - **Answer**: Because there is no **preventive maintenance schedule** in place for the temperature control system.

Conclusion from the 5 Whys Process

By asking "Why" five times, the team discovers that the root cause of the high scrap rate is not just the **inconsistent temperatures** on the extruder lines, but specifically the **lack of a preventive maintenance schedule** for the temperature control system. Without regular calibration, the system drifts out of the optimal range, leading to high temperatures, which in turn causes the pipes to become brittle and uneven in thickness.

Implementing Solutions Based on the 5 Whys

Once the root cause has been identified, the team can implement targeted solutions to prevent the problem from recurring. In this case, the solutions should focus on ensuring the **temperature control system** is properly maintained and calibrated, thereby preventing temperature fluctuations.

Proposed Solutions:

1. **Create a Preventive Maintenance Schedule**: Implement a regular maintenance plan for the temperature control system to ensure it stays calibrated and functional.
   - **Action**: The maintenance team will perform monthly checks on the system, calibrating the sensors and verifying that the system operates within the set temperature limits.
2. **Automate Temperature Monitoring**: Install an automated temperature control system that continuously monitors and adjusts the temperature without the need for manual intervention.
   - **Action**: An automated system will maintain the temperature within a **±2°C range** of the target, eliminating fluctuations that lead to defects.
3. **Operator Training**: Train operators on how to use the new automated temperature control system and how to detect early signs of malfunction.
   - **Action**: Conduct workshops for operators on how to monitor and respond to system alerts, reducing manual interventions and ensuring consistent operations.

Benefits of the 5 Whys Process

The **5 Whys** method provides several key benefits, particularly when used in a manufacturing environment:

1. **Simplicity**: The method is easy to implement and does not require complex tools or advanced knowledge, making it accessible to all employees.
2. **Focus on Root Cause**: By pushing past superficial symptoms, the 5 Whys method ensures that teams address the **real problem**, leading to lasting solutions rather than quick fixes.
3. **Prevents Recurrence**: Solutions that address root causes are more effective at preventing the issue from recurring, improving long-term performance and reducing waste.
4. **Team Collaboration**: The 5 Whys encourages teams to collaborate, bringing different perspectives together to fully understand the problem.
5. **Supports Continuous Improvement**: The method is integral to **continuous improvement** practices like **Lean** and **Six Sigma**, helping organizations continually refine processes and eliminate inefficiencies.

Common Pitfalls and How to Avoid Them

While the **5 Whys** is a highly effective tool, it can sometimes be misused or oversimplified. Here are some common pitfalls and how to avoid them:

1. Stopping Too Soon:

Sometimes teams stop asking "Why" after two or three levels of questioning, which leads to shallow solutions that don't fully address the root cause. It's essential to keep pushing until the actual cause is identified.

- **Tip**: Always aim for at least **five levels** of questioning, but be prepared to ask more if needed.

2. Lack of Data:

If teams rely solely on assumptions instead of data to answer the "Whys," they may misidentify the root cause.

- **Tip**: Use **data** and **evidence** to support each answer. For example, verify that temperature fluctuations are linked to scrap rates using historical data before proceeding.

3. Blaming People Instead of Processes:

Focusing too much on human error rather than process failures can lead to solutions that blame individuals rather than improving systems.

- **Tip**: Focus on **processes, systems, and workflows**, not individuals. Even if human error is involved, the solution should involve creating systems that prevent such errors from occurring in the future.

4. Treating Symptoms:

Teams may mistakenly treat symptoms (e.g., fixing broken equipment) without addressing why the symptoms occurred (e.g., lack of maintenance).

- **Tip**: Ensure that the 5 Whys process leads to solutions that address the **underlying causes** of the problem, not just the immediate issues.

Conclusion: The Power of the 5 Whys in Root Cause Analysis

The **5 Whys** is a fundamental tool in problem-solving methodologies like **Lean** and **Six Sigma**. Its simplicity and effectiveness make it accessible for anyone looking to identify the **root cause** of a problem. By repeatedly asking "Why?" teams can move beyond superficial symptoms and uncover the deeper issues that are causing inefficiencies, defects, or delays.

In the case of the **polyethylene pipe manufacturing factory**, the 5 Whys helped the team discover that the high scrap rate was caused by **temperature control issues** due to the **lack of a preventive maintenance schedule**. Armed with this knowledge, they implemented solutions that not only corrected the immediate problem but also prevented future occurrences.

The 5 Whys process is an invaluable tool for driving **continuous improvement** and eliminating the root causes of problems in any organization, ensuring that improvements are both sustainable and impactful.

Chapter 10: Defects Per Million Opportunities (DPMO) – Measuring Process Quality in Six Sigma

Introduction to DPMO

Defects Per Million Opportunities (DPMO) is an important metric used in **Six Sigma** to measure the quality of a manufacturing or business process. It provides a way to express how many defects occur in a process for every one million opportunities for a defect to happen. DPMO helps us understand how consistent a process is and how often it might make mistakes. The ultimate goal in Six Sigma is to reduce defects to an incredibly low number, which helps achieve **better quality**, **lower costs**, and **higher customer satisfaction**.

In this chapter, we will explore what DPMO is, its origins in **Six Sigma**, and how it helps manufacturers and businesses improve their operations. We'll also look at how DPMO fits into the **broader history** of quality management and why it's a powerful tool for continuous improvement.

The History of DPMO and Six Sigma

Six Sigma was developed in the 1980s by **Motorola**, a major American electronics company. At that time, Motorola faced challenges with inconsistent product quality and high defect rates, leading to customer dissatisfaction and increased production costs. In response, the company began searching for ways to dramatically improve the quality of its products by reducing the number of errors in its processes.

Bill Smith, an engineer at Motorola, along with other quality experts, began developing a strategy to identify and reduce defects systematically. They eventually created **Six Sigma** as a structured approach to improving quality. The term "**Six Sigma**" itself refers to the **six standard deviations** between the mean of a process and its acceptable limits, with the goal of achieving almost no defects—**3.4 defects per million opportunities**.

One of the key metrics they introduced was **DPMO**. By measuring how many errors occurred in a process for every **one million opportunities**, Motorola and other companies that adopted Six Sigma could clearly see how far they needed to improve to reach the **Six Sigma standard** of quality. DPMO became a benchmark for understanding the performance of a process, helping to quantify quality in a clear and consistent way.

Understanding Defects Per Million Opportunities (DPMO)

To understand **DPMO**, let's break down what it means in simple terms:

- A **defect** is anything that doesn't meet customer requirements or expectations. For example, in manufacturing polyethylene pipes, defects might include pipes that are too thin, too short, or have cracks.
- An **opportunity** is any point where something can go wrong. In a product, each characteristic (like diameter, length, or surface smoothness) is an opportunity for a defect to occur.

DPMO measures how many of these defects occur out of one million chances for a defect to happen. It provides a detailed way to see how often errors occur and helps companies set goals to reduce those errors over time.

Example: Calculating DPMO

Imagine that a factory produces **1,000 polyethylene pipes**, and each pipe has **3 critical features** (e.g., diameter, thickness, length) that could potentially have defects. This gives us a total of **3,000 opportunities for defects** (since there are 3 features for each of the 1,000 pipes). If **15 defects** are found during quality inspection, the DPMO can be calculated as follows:

1. **Calculate the Total Opportunities for Defects**:

$$\text{Total Opportunities} = \text{Number of Units} \times \text{Number of Opportunities per Unit} = 1,000 \times 3 = 3,000$$

2. **Calculate DPMO**:

$$\text{DPMO} = \left(\frac{\text{Number of Defects}}{\text{Total Opportunities}}\right) \times 1,000,000$$

$$\text{DPMO} = \left(\frac{15}{3,000}\right) \times 1,000,000 = 5,000$$

So, the factory's DPMO is **5,000**, which means that there are **5,000 defects per one million opportunities**.

Why is DPMO Important in Manufacturing and Business?

DPMO is valuable because it provides a clear, standardized way to measure the performance of a process. This measurement can be applied across different industries, from manufacturing to healthcare, allowing companies to track and improve quality.

1. Establishing Quality Benchmarks

- DPMO allows companies to **benchmark** their performance against industry standards or other processes within the organization.
- It is also a way to measure improvement. By comparing DPMO scores over time, companies can see if their changes have made a positive impact.

2. Setting Improvement Goals

- A lower **DPMO** means fewer defects and a more reliable process.
- Many companies strive to achieve a **DPMO** that corresponds to a **Six Sigma level**, which means only **3.4 defects per million opportunities**. This level of quality is associated with near-perfect performance and results in better customer satisfaction and lower production costs.

3. Easy Comparison Across Processes

- Because DPMO is a standard measure, it allows companies to easily compare **different processes**. For example, if one production line has a DPMO of **10,000** and another has **50,000**, it's clear that the first production line is much more efficient and consistent.

4. Reducing Costs and Increasing Customer Satisfaction

- Fewer defects mean fewer products that need to be **reworked**, **repaired**, or **scrapped**, leading to **cost savings**.
- **Higher quality** also means **happier customers**, as they are more likely to receive products that meet their expectations, reducing the chances of complaints or returns.

DPMO and the Sigma Level

Sigma levels are used to measure the capability of a process in terms of how many defects it produces. The higher the sigma level, the fewer defects there are. **Six Sigma** corresponds to **3.4 defects per million opportunities**, which is very close to perfect quality.

Here is a quick look at **sigma levels** and their corresponding **DPMO values**:

- **2 Sigma**: About **308,537 defects per million opportunities**.
- **3 Sigma**: About **66,807 defects per million opportunities**.
- **4 Sigma**: About **6,210 defects per million opportunities**.
- **5 Sigma**: About **233 defects per million opportunities**.
- **6 Sigma**: **3.4 defects per million opportunities** (almost perfect quality).

Most companies start somewhere around **3 Sigma**, meaning that there is significant room for improvement. The goal is to use **Six Sigma tools** like **DMAIC (Define, Measure, Analyze, Improve, Control)** to systematically reduce variability and improve the process over time, moving closer to a **Six Sigma level**.

How Does DPMO Drive Continuous Improvement?

Continuous improvement is at the heart of Six Sigma, and DPMO plays a vital role in measuring and guiding these efforts. Here's how:

1. Data-Driven Decisions

- By calculating **DPMO**, companies use actual data to understand how well their processes are performing. Instead of guessing, they can see exactly where improvements are needed and track progress in reducing defects.

2. Identifying Opportunities for Kaizen

- **Kaizen** refers to small, ongoing changes aimed at improving processes. High DPMO values help identify areas that need Kaizen efforts, allowing teams to target their improvements where they will have the biggest impact.

3. Using PDCA for Improvement Cycles

- Once a high **DPMO** is identified, companies can use the **PDCA (Plan-Do-Check-Act)** cycle to reduce defects. This involves:
    - **Plan**: Identifying the problem (high DPMO) and planning changes to address it.
    - **Do**: Implementing the change on a small scale.
    - **Check**: Measuring the impact of the change on the DPMO.

- o **Act**: If the change is successful, applying it across the entire process and updating standard procedures.

4. Standard Operating Procedures (SOPs) to Sustain Improvements

- After reducing DPMO, it's important to **sustain** the improvements. This is often done by updating **Standard Operating Procedures (SOPs)** to ensure that new, better methods are consistently applied.

DPMO in Action: A Manufacturing Example

Let's imagine a factory that makes **plastic caps** for bottles. Initially, they calculate a DPMO of **20,000**, meaning there are 20,000 defects per million opportunities. Some of the common defects include caps that don't fit, are chipped, or have a rough finish.

By applying **Six Sigma tools**:

1. They identify the **root causes** of the defects (e.g., inconsistent machine temperature and poor material quality).
2. The team conducts **Kaizen events** to standardize temperature settings and ensure better material quality.
3. The process is tracked and **DPMO** is recalculated after improvements.

After implementing the changes, the DPMO drops to **5,000**. This reduction means the process is now much more consistent, resulting in fewer defective caps, lower production costs, and happier customers.

Conclusion: The Role of DPMO in Achieving Six Sigma Quality

Defects Per Million Opportunities (DPMO) is a powerful way to measure how well a process is performing. It gives a clear picture of how often defects occur and helps manufacturers understand where they need to improve.

By reducing **DPMO**, companies can move closer to achieving **Six Sigma** quality, which means fewer errors, lower costs, and higher customer satisfaction. DPMO is not just a number—it is a tool for **continuous improvement**, helping to guide teams toward making better decisions, implementing changes, and sustaining improvements over time. In today's competitive world, measuring and reducing DPMO is key to achieving high-quality products that meet customer needs effectively.

Chapter 11: Kanban System – A Visual Approach to Workflow Management

Introduction to the Kanban System

The **Kanban system** is a Lean workflow management method designed to improve **efficiency, reduce waste**, and **optimize processes**. Kanban originated in **Toyota's manufacturing system** in the 1940s as a way to manage inventory levels and ensure that production was aligned with demand. The word **"kanban"** in Japanese means **"visual signal"** or **"card,"** and it refers to the physical or digital cards used to signal the need for materials or work to move through a process.

Today, Kanban is widely used not just in manufacturing but also in various industries like software development, healthcare, and logistics. It provides a **visual representation** of work items as they move through stages of production, ensuring that the right tasks are done at the right time, with minimal waste and delays.

In this chapter, we'll explore how the **Kanban system** can be applied to improve the workflow on the **extruder lines** of a **polyethylene pipe manufacturing factory**, helping the team optimize inventory levels, reduce waiting times, and enhance overall productivity.

Principles of the Kanban System

The Kanban system is built on several core principles:

1. Visualizing Work

Kanban uses visual tools (such as boards and cards) to make work items and their status visible to the entire team. This ensures transparency and allows team members to quickly understand what stage of production each task or material is in.

2. Limiting Work in Progress (WIP)

To prevent bottlenecks, Kanban sets limits on how much work can be in progress at any given time. By doing this, it ensures that the team completes existing tasks before taking on new ones, leading to a more balanced and manageable workflow.

3. Managing Flow

Kanban helps teams focus on managing the flow of work from start to finish, ensuring that work moves smoothly and efficiently through each stage of the process.

4. Making Process Policies Explicit

For Kanban to work effectively, the team must establish clear rules and policies about how work moves from one stage to another. This helps create a predictable and structured workflow.

5. Continuous Improvement

Kanban encourages regular feedback and continuous improvement (known as **Kaizen** in Lean). By monitoring the flow of work and identifying inefficiencies, teams can make incremental changes to enhance productivity.

How the Kanban System Works

The basic Kanban system consists of three key components:

1. **Kanban Cards**: Each card represents a task, item, or work order. These cards move through various stages of the process to signal the progress of work.
2. **Kanban Board**: A board is used to visually display the status of each Kanban card. The board is divided into columns, each representing a specific stage of the process (e.g., "To Do," "In Progress," "Completed").
3. **Work-in-Progress (WIP) Limits**: Each column on the board may have a limit on the number of tasks that can be in progress at one time, preventing bottlenecks and overloading.

Let's explore how the **polyethylene pipe manufacturing factory** can implement a **Kanban system** to optimize production on the extruder lines, where **high scrap rates** have been observed due to inefficiencies in temperature control, inventory management, and work sequencing.

Applying Kanban to the Extruder Line Process

In the factory's current setup, the production process is facing issues with **inventory overload**, **long waiting times**, and **frequent downtime**. This results in an inconsistent workflow, where materials pile up in some stages while others remain underutilized. The team can use Kanban to smooth out this process, ensuring that materials, tasks, and production stages are better aligned with demand.

Step 1: Designing a Kanban Board for the Extruder Line

The first step is to create a **Kanban board** that represents the stages of the extrusion process. Each stage of production should have its own column, and each work item (e.g., a batch of pipes) should have a **Kanban card** that moves across the board as the work progresses.

Example Kanban Board Layout for the Extruder Line:

Column	Description
Raw Materials Available	Indicates that raw polyethylene pellets are available for use.
Extrusion Scheduled	Pipes have been scheduled for production on the extruder lines.
Extrusion in Progress	The extruder is currently producing pipes.
Cooling/Inspection	Pipes are cooling and being inspected for defects.
Completed Pipes	Pipes have passed inspection and are ready for shipment.

Step 2: Creating Kanban Cards for Each Batch

Each batch of pipes produced on the extruder line will have a **Kanban card**. This card contains all relevant information about the batch, such as the batch number, material specifications, target temperature settings, and the quantity of pipes to be produced.

- **Card Information**:
  - **Batch Number**: #12345
  - **Material Type**: Polyethylene (High-Density)

- **Target Temperature**: 220°C–230°C
- **Quantity**: 500 pipes
- **Scheduled Time**: 4 hours

These cards will move across the **Kanban board** as the batch progresses through different stages, from raw materials to completed pipes.

Step 3: Setting Work-in-Progress (WIP) Limits

One of the key aspects of Kanban is setting **WIP limits** to ensure that the factory does not overload any stage of the process. For example, if too many batches are in progress at the **Extrusion in Progress** stage, it could overwhelm the extruder line and cause delays, leading to **waiting waste**.

- **Example WIP Limit**: The **Extrusion in Progress** column can have a WIP limit of **2 batches**. This means that only two batches can be in production at the same time, preventing the team from overloading the extruder line and creating a bottleneck.

Step 4: Using Kanban to Manage Raw Materials

In the current process, the factory often has too many raw materials (polyethylene pellets) stored in inventory, leading to **inventory waste**. The Kanban system can help reduce excess inventory by signaling when new materials are needed **just in time**.

- **Kanban Signal for Raw Materials**: When the **Raw Materials Available** column is nearly empty, the Kanban system signals to the warehouse team to replenish materials. This ensures that raw materials are only delivered to the production floor when needed, reducing excess storage and keeping the workflow smooth.

Benefits of Implementing Kanban on the Extruder Lines

By applying the Kanban system to the extruder lines, the factory can achieve several important benefits:

1. Smoother Workflow

The visual nature of the **Kanban board** ensures that the entire team can see where each batch is in the production process. This allows them to easily identify bottlenecks and areas of improvement. For example, if too many cards are stuck in the **Cooling/Inspection** stage, it may indicate that quality control is taking too long and needs to be optimized.

2. Reduced Inventory and Overproduction

By setting WIP limits and managing material flow based on **demand**, the factory can prevent overproduction and reduce excess inventory. The Kanban system ensures that **raw materials** are delivered when needed and that production is aligned with customer demand, reducing the need to store large quantities of unused materials.

3. Reduced Waiting Times

By optimizing the flow of work and ensuring that no stage is overloaded, Kanban reduces **waiting waste**. With clear WIP limits, the extruder lines are not held up waiting for downstream processes to catch up. This helps reduce overall production lead time and improve the efficiency of the extruder lines.

4. Improved Process Visibility

The Kanban board provides a **real-time visual representation** of what's happening in production. Both managers and operators can quickly assess the status of each batch and identify areas where intervention may be needed. This increases **transparency** and helps with **decision-making**.

5. Enhanced Responsiveness to Changes

Kanban is a **flexible system** that allows for quick adjustments based on demand changes. If a customer needs an urgent order of pipes, the team can prioritize that batch by moving its Kanban card to the top of the **Extrusion Scheduled** column, ensuring it gets produced quickly without disrupting the flow of other batches.

Continuous Improvement with Kanban

A key principle of Kanban is **continuous improvement** (Kaizen). The Kanban system is not static; it should evolve as the team learns more about its processes and identifies areas for optimization. By analyzing the data from the Kanban board (such as how long each batch spends in each stage), the team can continuously refine and improve the process.

1. Regularly Review WIP Limits

As the factory becomes more efficient, WIP limits can be adjusted. For example, if the **Extrusion in Progress** stage consistently finishes ahead of schedule, the team might increase the WIP limit from 2 to 3 batches, allowing more work to be processed at the same time without creating bottlenecks.

2. Identify Bottlenecks

The Kanban board helps identify bottlenecks in the production process. For example, if many cards are stuck in the **Cooling/Inspection** stage, it may indicate that the inspection process is slowing down production. The team can then investigate and implement solutions, such as adding more inspectors or automating parts of the inspection process.

3. Track Lead Time

By measuring how long it takes for a card to move from the **Raw Materials Available** stage to the **Completed Pipes** stage, the team can track **lead time**. If lead time is longer than expected, it may signal inefficiencies or bottlenecks that need to be addressed.

Digital Kanban Systems

While traditional Kanban systems are often physical boards with sticky notes or cards, many companies today use **digital Kanban boards**. These digital tools offer additional advantages, such as:

- **Real-time updates**: Team members can instantly see changes to the workflow, regardless of their location.
- **Data tracking**: Digital Kanban boards can automatically track cycle times, lead times, and bottlenecks, providing valuable insights into process efficiency.
- **Integration with other systems**: Digital tools can integrate with other business systems like ERP (Enterprise Resource Planning) or MRP (Material Requirements Planning) systems, ensuring seamless coordination between different functions.

Some popular digital Kanban tools include **Trello, Jira,** and **Kanbanize**.

Conclusion: The Kanban System as a Tool for Workflow Optimization

The **Kanban system** provides a structured, visual way to manage and optimize workflows, making it an essential tool for any manufacturing process. By implementing Kanban on the **extruder lines** of the **polyethylene pipe manufacturing factory**, the team can improve **workflow efficiency**, **reduce waste**, and **minimize waiting times**, all while ensuring that production is aligned with demand.

Kanban's **visual nature** and focus on **limiting work in progress** make it easy to identify bottlenecks and areas for improvement. By regularly reviewing the Kanban board, adjusting WIP limits, and engaging in **continuous improvement**, the factory can maintain a smooth, efficient production process that meets customer needs while minimizing waste.

The flexibility of the Kanban system also ensures that the factory can quickly respond to changes in demand, making it an invaluable tool for **Lean manufacturing** and **just-in-time production**.

Chapter 12: SMED – Single-Minute Exchange of Dies: Reducing Changeover Time for Maximum Efficiency

Introduction to SMED

Single-Minute Exchange of Dies (SMED) is a **Lean manufacturing technique** that focuses on dramatically reducing the time it takes to switch between tasks or product lines, especially in processes that require machine setup or tool changes. The goal of SMED is to cut down **changeover times** to less than 10 minutes—or **single digits**—to improve operational efficiency, reduce waste, and increase production flexibility.

SMED was developed by **Shigeo Shingo**, an industrial engineer who played a pivotal role in the development of the **Toyota Production System (TPS)**. SMED allows companies to produce smaller batches of products, enabling **just-in-time (JIT) production** and reducing the need for excess inventory.

In this chapter, we'll explore the **SMED methodology** in detail and how it can be applied to the **polyethylene pipe manufacturing factory**, particularly on the **extruder lines**, where reducing changeover times during **die changes** can significantly improve production efficiency and reduce downtime.

The Importance of SMED in Manufacturing

In many manufacturing processes, **changeover times** are a significant source of waste. A long changeover time can cause:

- **Excess downtime**: Machines remain idle while being reconfigured for the next production run.
- **Reduced flexibility**: Longer changeover times make it harder to adapt to changing customer demands.
- **Increased batch sizes**: To compensate for long changeovers, companies may produce larger batches than necessary, leading to excess inventory and associated costs.

By implementing SMED, companies can achieve:

- **Faster production**: Shorter changeover times increase equipment availability.
- **Smaller batch sizes**: Reduced setup times allow for more frequent changeovers, enabling companies to produce only what is needed.
- **Increased flexibility**: Faster changeovers allow for a greater variety of products to be produced in a shorter time frame.

The 4 Steps of the SMED Process

The SMED method can be broken down into **four key steps** that focus on simplifying and streamlining changeover activities. The goal is to move as many tasks as possible from **internal setup** (tasks that must be done while the machine is idle) to **external setup** (tasks that can be done while the machine is running), thereby minimizing downtime.

1. Separate Internal and External Setup

In this step, the first task is to **identify** which changeover activities are **internal** (must be performed while the machine is stopped) and which are **external** (can be done while the machine is running).

- **Internal Setup**: Any task that requires the machine to be idle (e.g., physically changing dies on the extruder line).
- **External Setup**: Tasks that can be performed while the machine is still running (e.g., preparing tools or materials in advance, fetching new dies before the machine stops).

Example in the Factory:

On the extruder lines, **internal setup** includes stopping the machine to physically change the **extrusion dies** when switching between different pipe sizes. **External setup** might involve gathering tools, inspecting the new dies, and preheating them while the current batch is still being produced.

2. Convert Internal Setup to External Setup

The next step is to **convert as many internal setup tasks** as possible into external ones. This is key to reducing downtime because it allows operators to perform tasks while the machine is still running, so the actual downtime is minimized.

Example in the Factory:

In the polyethylene pipe manufacturing process, **die preheating** can be done before the machine stops. By preparing the next set of dies in advance, the time spent waiting for dies to reach the correct temperature after the machine stops is eliminated.

3. Streamline Internal Setup

For tasks that **cannot be converted** into external setup, the goal is to **simplify and standardize** them so they can be performed more efficiently. This might involve using **quick-release mechanisms** or **standardized tools** to speed up the die change process.

Example in the Factory:

If die changes on the extruder lines require unscrewing multiple bolts, the factory could implement **quick-change die systems** that allow dies to be swapped out quickly using standardized fasteners, reducing the time spent during internal setup.

4. Eliminate Waste in All Setup Activities

Finally, eliminate any unnecessary steps or waste in both internal and external setup activities. Look for redundant actions, inefficient movements, or poorly organized workstations that slow down the process.

Example in the Factory:

By applying the **5S methodology** (Sort, Set in order, Shine, Standardize, Sustain), the team can organize tools and equipment at the die-change station to minimize the time spent searching for or retrieving necessary items during the setup process.

Implementing SMED in the Polyethylene Pipe Manufacturing Process

In our factory, the **extruder lines** produce various sizes and types of polyethylene pipes. Switching between different pipe diameters requires **die changes**, which currently take **30 to 45 minutes** per changeover. By applying SMED, the team aims to reduce changeover times to under **10 minutes**.

Step 1: Analyze the Current Changeover Process

The team first conducts a **time study** to document each step of the die change process. They identify which tasks are internal and which are external. For example:

- **Internal Setup**:
  o Stopping the machine to remove the current die.
  o Waiting for the new die to heat up after installation.
- **External Setup**:
  o Locating and retrieving the correct die.
  o Preheating the die while the machine is still running.

Step 2: Convert Internal Setup to External Setup

The team identifies tasks that can be done **before the machine stops**, converting internal tasks to external ones:

- **Preheat the new die** while the machine is still running with the old die. This allows the new die to be ready as soon as the old die is removed.
- **Stage the new die and tools** at the machine so they are ready for immediate use when the machine is stopped.

Step 3: Streamline Internal Setup Activities

For tasks that must still be performed while the machine is idle, the team works on **simplifying and speeding up** the process:

- Install **quick-release fasteners** on the extruder so that the old die can be removed and the new one installed in a matter of seconds, rather than requiring bolts to be unscrewed and screwed back in.

- Use **color-coded dies** and **tools** to ensure that the correct parts are easily identifiable and that no time is wasted searching for them.

Step 4: Eliminate Waste in the Setup Process

Using the **5S methodology**, the team organizes the **die change station** to ensure that all tools, dies, and equipment are kept in a designated location and are easy to access:

- **Set in Order**: Store dies and tools in specific locations near the extruder line, reducing the need to walk long distances to retrieve them.
- **Standardize**: Develop a **standard operating procedure (SOP)** for die changes that includes a checklist to ensure that all steps are completed efficiently and consistently.

SMED Example: Die Change on the Extruder Line

Let's walk through an example of a die change on the extruder line before and after implementing SMED.

Before SMED:

1. The machine is stopped to begin the die change.
2. The operator spends 5 minutes searching for the correct die and tools.
3. The operator removes the old die, taking 10 minutes.
4. The new die is installed but requires 15 minutes to reach the correct temperature.
5. The machine is restarted after a total of **45 minutes** of downtime.

After Implementing SMED:

1. The new die is **preheated** while the machine is still running, and tools are prepared at the workstation (external setup).
2. When the machine stops, the operator removes the old die using **quick-release fasteners** (internal setup), taking only **5 minutes**.
3. The preheated die is immediately installed, requiring no additional waiting time for heating.
4. The machine is restarted after a total of **10 minutes** of downtime.

Benefits of SMED in the Factory

By implementing SMED on the extruder lines, the factory can realize several important benefits:

1. Reduced Downtime

Reducing changeover times from **45 minutes to 10 minutes** allows the factory to increase machine availability and minimize idle time. This means more time is spent producing valuable products rather than waiting for setups to be completed.

2. Increased Flexibility

With faster changeovers, the factory can easily switch between different pipe sizes or product types. This supports **just-in-time production**, where the factory can produce smaller batches of products based on customer demand, reducing the need for excess inventory.

3. Lower Inventory Costs

Faster changeovers allow the factory to produce smaller, more frequent batches, which reduces the need to store large quantities of finished goods or raw materials. This helps minimize **inventory costs** and reduce the risk of overproduction.

4. Improved Productivity

By streamlining setup activities, operators can perform die changes more efficiently, reducing the overall labor required for each changeover. This boosts overall productivity and allows the factory to produce more output in the same amount of time.

5. Enhanced Quality

SMED encourages **standardization** of setup procedures, ensuring that die changes are performed consistently and correctly. This helps reduce errors and improves the quality of the pipes produced, reducing defects and scrap.

Challenges of Implementing SMED

While SMED can deliver significant improvements, there are some challenges that teams may encounter during implementation:

1. Resistance to Change

Operators may resist adopting new procedures, particularly if they are used to performing die changes in a certain way. It's important to involve the team in the SMED process from the beginning and ensure that they understand the benefits.

2. Upfront Investment

In some cases, implementing SMED may require **investment in new tools or equipment**, such as quick-release mechanisms or preheating systems. However, these costs are often quickly offset by the gains in efficiency and productivity.

3. Need for Continuous Improvement

SMED is not a one-time fix. The process must be continually monitored and refined to ensure that improvements are sustained and that new opportunities for efficiency gains are identified.

Measuring the Success of SMED

Once SMED has been implemented, it's important to track **key performance indicators (KPIs)** to measure its success. Some relevant KPIs include:

- **Changeover Time**: The time it takes to complete a full die change before and after SMED.
- **Overall Equipment Effectiveness (OEE)**: Measure improvements in equipment availability, performance, and quality after reducing changeover times.
- **Cycle Time**: Track how reducing changeover times affects the overall cycle time of production.
- **Productivity**: Measure increases in output or throughput as a result of faster changeovers.

Conclusion: SMED as a Tool for Lean Manufacturing

Single-Minute Exchange of Dies (SMED) is a powerful tool for reducing **downtime**, improving

efficiency, and increasing **production flexibility** in manufacturing processes. By breaking down the changeover process and systematically converting **internal setup** tasks to **external setup** tasks, manufacturers can dramatically reduce the time it takes to switch between different product lines or tasks.

In the **polyethylene pipe manufacturing factory**, applying SMED to the **extruder line** process enables faster die changes, reducing downtime from **45 minutes to under 10 minutes**. This results in more productive use of the extruder lines, lower inventory levels, and the ability to meet customer demand more effectively.

By continuously improving setup processes and eliminating waste, SMED helps manufacturers become more agile, responsive, and competitive in today's fast-paced marketplace.

Chapter 13: Just-In-Time (JIT) Production – Maximizing Efficiency and Reducing Waste

Introduction to Just-In-Time (JIT) Production

Just-In-Time (JIT) production is a **Lean manufacturing methodology** focused on producing exactly what is needed, **when it is needed**, and in the **quantities required**—no more, no less. The primary objective of JIT is to reduce **waste** and **increase efficiency** by minimizing inventory, improving production flow, and responding flexibly to customer demand.

JIT originated from the **Toyota Production System (TPS)** and was pioneered by **Taiichi Ohno** at Toyota in the 1950s. It revolutionized manufacturing by transforming the way companies manage inventory, production scheduling, and supplier relationships. JIT is based on **continuous improvement**, where manufacturers aim to improve quality and responsiveness while reducing costs.

In this chapter, we'll explore the principles of **JIT production** in detail and how it can be applied to a **polyethylene pipe manufacturing factory**. By adopting JIT principles, the factory can minimize **inventory costs**, reduce **production lead times**, and improve **overall efficiency** on the **extruder lines**.

The Core Principles of JIT Production

The JIT philosophy revolves around several core principles that drive its success. These principles work together to eliminate waste and optimize production flow:

1. Demand-Driven Production

JIT focuses on producing goods based on actual **customer demand**, not forecasts. This reduces the risk of overproduction and ensures that resources are only used when they are needed.

2. Inventory Reduction

By minimizing **raw material, work-in-progress (WIP),** and **finished goods inventory**, JIT reduces the costs associated with storing, managing, and maintaining excess stock. Inventory is considered waste in JIT, as it ties up capital and risks becoming obsolete.

3. Short Lead Times

JIT aims to shorten the time between receiving an order and delivering the finished product. By reducing lead times, manufacturers can be more responsive to changing customer demands and avoid delays.

4. Continuous Flow

A key element of JIT is creating a **continuous flow** of work, where materials and products move smoothly from one production stage to the next without interruptions or bottlenecks.

5. Supplier Relationships

JIT requires close coordination with suppliers to ensure that **raw materials** are delivered in small quantities, **just in time** for production. Reliable suppliers are critical to JIT success, as disruptions in the supply chain can halt production.

6. Waste Reduction

JIT aligns closely with **Lean manufacturing** by focusing on the **elimination of waste** in all forms, including excess inventory, waiting times, overproduction, and defects.

How JIT Works in a Manufacturing Environment

JIT production is often visualized through tools such as **Kanban**, which helps manage the flow of materials and production tasks. In a **polyethylene pipe manufacturing factory**, JIT would involve producing pipes based on actual customer orders, minimizing excess inventory, and ensuring that production is closely aligned with demand.

Example: Traditional vs. JIT Production

- **Traditional Production**: In a traditional manufacturing setup, the factory produces large batches of polyethylene pipes based on forecasts. Excess inventory is kept on hand in case of sudden demand surges, leading to higher storage costs and the risk of overproduction.
- **JIT Production**: In a JIT environment, the factory only produces pipes when there is an order from a customer. Raw materials (polyethylene pellets) are delivered **just in time** for production, and finished pipes are shipped out immediately, minimizing storage costs and reducing the risk of overproduction.

Applying JIT to the Polyethylene Pipe Manufacturing Process

In the **polyethylene pipe manufacturing factory**, the current challenge is managing **inventory** and **production flow** on the extruder lines, where excess inventory and long lead times lead to inefficiencies. By applying **JIT principles**, the factory can streamline production, reduce waste, and better meet customer demands.

Step 1: Align Production with Customer Demand

In JIT, production should only occur when there is actual **customer demand**. Instead of producing large batches of pipes in anticipation of future orders, the factory should focus on producing **smaller batches** based on real-time orders. This ensures that production is driven by actual demand rather than forecasts.

JIT Example in the Factory:

- **Current State**: The factory produces **large batches** of pipes (10,000 units) based on demand forecasts, leading to excess finished goods inventory.
- **JIT Approach**: Instead of producing 10,000 pipes at once, the factory produces smaller batches of 2,000 units based on customer orders. This reduces the amount of finished goods inventory and ensures that production is closely aligned with real-time demand.

Step 2: Minimize Inventory Levels

One of the core principles of JIT is to **minimize inventory** at every stage of production. Excess inventory ties up capital, increases storage costs, and risks becoming obsolete if customer preferences change. In the **polyethylene pipe manufacturing factory**, this means reducing the amount of raw materials (polyethylene pellets), work-in-progress (WIP), and finished pipes in storage.

JIT Inventory Management Example:

- **Current State**: The factory maintains **large inventories** of polyethylene pellets and finished pipes to ensure that production can continue uninterrupted.
- **JIT Approach**: The factory works with suppliers to deliver **small quantities** of polyethylene pellets just as they are needed for production. Finished pipes are shipped out immediately after production, with minimal time spent in storage.

Step 3: Shorten Lead Times

By reducing setup times (using methods like **SMED**) and optimizing the flow of materials, JIT allows manufacturers to **shorten lead times**—the time it takes to produce and deliver a product. Short lead times are critical in a JIT system, as they enable the factory to respond quickly to changing customer demands.

Lead Time Reduction Example:

- **Current State**: The current lead time from receiving an order to shipping finished pipes is **4 weeks** due to long changeover times on the extruder lines and delays in material handling.
- **JIT Approach**: By implementing **SMED** to reduce changeover times and using **Kanban** to manage material flow, the factory reduces lead times to **2 weeks**.

Step 4: Implement a Continuous Flow

JIT emphasizes the creation of a **continuous flow** where materials and products move smoothly through each stage of production. In the factory, this means ensuring that polyethylene pellets are delivered just in time for extrusion, and that finished pipes move seamlessly to packaging and shipping without bottlenecks or delays.

Continuous Flow Example:

- **Current State**: Raw materials are delivered in bulk and stored in large quantities, often resulting in delays when retrieving them for production. Finished pipes sit in storage until there is space available in the shipping department.
- **JIT Approach**: Materials are delivered in small batches to match the production schedule, and finished pipes are immediately moved from the extruder line to the shipping department, ensuring a smooth and continuous flow of work.

Step 5: Build Strong Supplier Relationships

JIT relies heavily on **reliable suppliers** who can deliver materials **on time** and in the required quantities. The factory must work closely with suppliers of **polyethylene pellets** to establish delivery schedules that align with production needs. Any disruption in the supply chain could halt production, so maintaining strong relationships and backup plans is critical.

Supplier Collaboration Example:

- **Current State**: The factory places bulk orders for polyethylene pellets every month, resulting in high

storage costs and the risk of material shortages if demand changes.
- **JIT Approach**: The factory establishes a **just-in-time delivery agreement** with suppliers, where smaller quantities of polyethylene pellets are delivered more frequently (e.g., weekly or bi-weekly) to match production schedules.

JIT Tools and Techniques

JIT is supported by several Lean tools and techniques that help ensure smooth production flow and inventory management. Some of the key tools include:

1. Kanban

As discussed in Chapter 10, **Kanban** is a visual system that helps manage and signal the need for materials and tasks. In a JIT system, **Kanban cards** are used to signal when materials need to be replenished or when work should proceed to the next stage.

Example: The factory uses a Kanban board to signal when polyethylene pellets should be delivered to the extruder lines. When the supply of pellets drops below a certain level, a Kanban card is sent to the supplier to trigger the next delivery.

2. Takt Time

Takt time is the rate at which products must be produced to meet customer demand. It ensures that production is synchronized with customer requirements and that no excess inventory is produced.

Example: If the factory has a customer order of 5,000 pipes to be delivered in 10 days, the takt time would be calculated as:

$$\text{Takt Time} = \frac{\text{Available Production Time}}{\text{Customer Demand}} = \frac{10 \text{ days}}{5000 \text{ pipes}} = 500 \text{ pipes/day}$$

The factory should aim to produce 500 pipes per day to meet the customer demand without overproduction.

3. SMED (Single-Minute Exchange of Dies)

As discussed in Chapter 11, **SMED** is a technique used to reduce setup times and minimize downtime during changeovers. SMED supports JIT by enabling quicker transitions between product types, reducing batch sizes, and increasing flexibility.

Benefits of Implementing JIT Production

By implementing JIT principles in the **polyethylene pipe manufacturing factory**, the team can achieve several key benefits:

1. Reduced Inventory Costs

One of the biggest advantages of JIT is the **reduction in inventory** at every stage of production. By only producing what is needed and reducing excess raw material and finished goods inventory, the factory can free up working capital, lower storage costs, and reduce the risk of obsolescence.

2. Improved Production Efficiency

JIT streamlines production by creating a **continuous flow** of materials and products, reducing waiting times and bottlenecks. This leads to improved **equipment**

utilization and shorter **lead times**, enabling the factory to respond quickly to customer demand.

3. Increased Product Quality

By focusing on producing smaller batches and reducing **overproduction**, JIT encourages a focus on **quality**. Operators have more time to inspect products and catch defects early, leading to higher first-pass yields and fewer defects.

4. Enhanced Flexibility

JIT allows the factory to be more responsive to changing customer demands. By reducing setup times and inventory levels, the factory can quickly adjust production to meet new orders or changes in product specifications.

5. Lower Production Costs

The reduction in waste, excess inventory, and lead times results in lower overall production costs. With fewer resources tied up in storage and less downtime during changeovers, the factory can operate more efficiently and at a lower cost.

Challenges of Implementing JIT Production

While JIT offers significant benefits, there are some challenges that manufacturers must address:

1. Supplier Reliability

JIT relies on the timely delivery of raw materials. Any disruption in the supply chain—such as a delay from a supplier—can halt production. Building strong relationships with reliable suppliers is critical to the success of JIT.

2. Demand Variability

If customer demand is unpredictable or fluctuates significantly, it can be difficult to maintain a JIT system. Manufacturers must have flexible production processes and the ability to quickly scale production up or down in response to demand changes.

3. Risk of Stockouts

With minimal inventory on hand, JIT increases the risk of **stockouts**—running out of materials before the next delivery arrives. Manufacturers must carefully manage inventory levels and coordinate with suppliers to avoid production disruptions.

Measuring the Success of JIT Production

Once JIT is implemented, it's important to measure its success by tracking key performance indicators (KPIs). Some relevant KPIs for JIT include:

1. Inventory Turnover

Inventory turnover measures how many times inventory is used or sold within a given period. A higher turnover rate indicates that the factory is effectively managing its inventory levels and reducing excess stock.

2. Lead Time

Lead time tracks how long it takes to complete a product from the moment an order is received to the time it is delivered. Reducing lead time is a key objective of JIT, as it allows the factory to respond more quickly to customer demand.

3. On-Time Delivery

On-time delivery measures the percentage of customer orders that are delivered by the agreed-upon date. By shortening lead times and improving production flow, JIT should result in higher on-time delivery rates.

4. First Pass Yield (FPY)

First pass yield measures the percentage of products that are manufactured correctly the first time without needing rework or repair. JIT encourages higher quality by reducing overproduction and focusing on smaller batches, which should lead to improvements in FPY.

Conclusion: The Power of JIT in Modern Manufacturing

Just-In-Time (JIT) production is a powerful tool for **streamlining manufacturing processes**, **reducing waste**, and **improving efficiency**. By producing only what is needed, when it is needed, JIT aligns production with actual demand, minimizing excess inventory and lowering costs.

In the **polyethylene pipe manufacturing factory**, implementing JIT principles can help reduce inventory levels, shorten lead times, and ensure that production is tightly aligned with customer orders. By focusing on continuous improvement and waste reduction, JIT allows manufacturers to operate more efficiently and remain competitive in today's fast-paced market.

While JIT presents some challenges—such as the need for reliable suppliers and the risk of stockouts—these can be overcome with careful planning, strong supplier relationships, and flexible production systems. Ultimately, JIT provides manufacturers with the tools they need to deliver **high-quality products**, **quickly**, and **efficiently**, while minimizing waste and maximizing value.

Chapter 14: Standard Operating Procedures (SOPs) – Establishing Consistency and Quality in Manufacturing

Introduction to Standard Operating Procedures (SOPs)

Standard Operating Procedures (SOPs) are detailed, written instructions designed to ensure that employees consistently perform tasks or processes **correctly**, **efficiently**, and **safely**. SOPs are crucial in **manufacturing**, where maintaining **quality**, **compliance**, and **productivity** is essential. SOPs provide a structured framework for workers to follow, reducing variability, minimizing errors, and ensuring that best practices are applied across all levels of the operation.

In a manufacturing environment, SOPs help standardize processes, from **equipment operation** and **quality control** to **safety measures** and **maintenance routines**. In this chapter, we will explore the importance of **SOPs** and how they can be applied to the **polyethylene pipe manufacturing factory** to improve consistency, reduce errors, and maintain high standards of quality on the **extruder lines**.

The Importance of SOPs in Manufacturing

SOPs serve several important purposes in manufacturing:

1. Consistency

SOPs ensure that tasks are performed the same way, regardless of who is completing the task. This standardization reduces variability and helps maintain a consistent level of quality across shifts and operators.

2. Quality Control

Well-documented SOPs help maintain **high product quality** by ensuring that processes are followed correctly. They provide clear guidelines for operators to follow, reducing the likelihood of defects and rework.

3. Compliance

In many industries, SOPs are essential for **regulatory compliance**. They help ensure that the manufacturing process meets industry standards and regulatory requirements, such as **ISO certifications** or **FDA** guidelines.

4. Training and Onboarding

SOPs are valuable tools for training new employees. By documenting each step of a process, SOPs provide a comprehensive resource that helps new workers quickly learn how to perform tasks correctly.

5. Safety

In potentially hazardous environments like manufacturing, SOPs include detailed instructions on how to safely operate machinery and handle materials, ensuring compliance with safety regulations and reducing the risk of accidents.

6. Continuous Improvement

SOPs provide a foundation for **continuous improvement** efforts, such as **Lean** and **Six Sigma** initiatives. By documenting the current process, the team can identify inefficiencies or areas for improvement and update SOPs accordingly.

Elements of a Well-Written SOP

A well-structured SOP should be **clear**, **concise**, and **easy to follow**. The following elements are typically included in a comprehensive SOP:

1. Title and Purpose

The title clearly defines the task or process covered by the SOP. The purpose section explains why the procedure is necessary, highlighting its significance in achieving specific objectives, such as maintaining product quality or ensuring safety.

- **Example Title: Extruder Line Setup and Operation for Polyethylene Pipes**
- **Example Purpose**: This SOP outlines the steps required to properly set up and operate the extruder lines for polyethylene pipe production, ensuring consistent quality and minimal defects.

2. Scope

The scope defines **who the SOP applies to** and **what tasks** are covered. It specifies which departments, processes, or personnel are responsible for following the SOP.

- **Example Scope**: This SOP applies to all operators and technicians responsible for setting up, running, and monitoring the extruder lines in the polyethylene pipe manufacturing department.

3. Responsibilities

This section defines the **roles and responsibilities** of individuals involved in the process. It outlines who is responsible for specific tasks, decisions, or approvals.

- **Example Responsibilities**:
  - **Operators**: Set up and operate the extruder line according to the SOP.
  - **Supervisors**: Ensure that operators are trained on the SOP and that the SOP is followed correctly.
  - **Maintenance Technicians**: Perform regular checks and maintenance as outlined in the SOP.

4. Equipment and Materials

List all the **equipment** and **materials** needed to perform the task. This ensures that the necessary tools are available and ready before starting the process.

- **Example Equipment**:
  - Extruder machine
  - Temperature control system
  - Preheater for extrusion dies
  - Polyethylene pellets

5. Step-by-Step Procedure

This section provides detailed, **step-by-step instructions** for completing the task. The instructions should be easy to understand, free of jargon, and follow a logical sequence. If appropriate, include diagrams or illustrations to clarify complex steps.

Example Step-by-Step Procedure:

1. **Prepare Materials**: Gather all necessary tools and materials, including the correct die for the pipe size and the preheated polyethylene pellets.
2. **Set Temperature Controls**: Adjust the extruder temperature to 220°C–230°C based on material specifications.
3. **Install the Die**: Install the die using the quick-release mechanism and ensure it is properly aligned.
4. **Start the Extrusion Process**: Begin the extrusion process, monitoring temperature and pressure to ensure consistency.
5. **Inspect First Output**: Inspect the first pipe produced for quality. If defects are present, adjust temperature or pressure accordingly.
6. **Monitor Production**: Continuously monitor the extruder for any signs of malfunction or variability in temperature or material flow.

6. Quality Control and Inspection

Include specific checkpoints for **quality control**, such as when inspections should occur or which aspects of the product should be evaluated. This ensures that defects are identified early and corrective actions can be taken before production continues.

- **Example Quality Control Section**:
  - **Pipe Thickness Check**: Every 30 minutes, measure the wall thickness of the pipe using a caliper and record the results.

- **Surface Inspection**: Inspect the surface of each pipe for imperfections (e.g., rough texture, warping) and note any abnormalities in the production log.

7. Safety Guidelines

List the **safety precautions** necessary to perform the task safely, including personal protective equipment (PPE) requirements, hazard warnings, and emergency procedures.

- **Example Safety Section**:
  - **PPE Requirements**: All operators must wear gloves, safety goggles, and heat-resistant clothing while handling the extruder.
  - **Emergency Stop**: In case of equipment malfunction, press the emergency stop button and notify the supervisor immediately.
  - **Temperature Warnings**: Avoid direct contact with heated parts of the extruder and dies.

8. Recordkeeping

Define the **documentation requirements** for the task, such as production logs, maintenance checklists, or quality inspection reports. This ensures accountability and provides a trail for tracking performance and compliance.

- **Example Recordkeeping Section**:
  - **Production Log**: Record the start and stop times of each batch, the number of pipes produced, and any issues encountered during production.
  - **Quality Check Log**: Record the results of the wall thickness measurements and any defects identified during inspections.

9. Review and Revision Process

SOPs must be **regularly reviewed** and **updated** to ensure they remain relevant and accurate. Include a section that details the process for reviewing and revising the SOP, as well as who is responsible for updates.

Example Review Section:

- **Review Frequency**: This SOP must be reviewed annually or when changes to the equipment, materials, or processes occur.
- **Responsible Party**: The production supervisor is responsible for reviewing and updating this SOP in collaboration with the quality control department.

Creating SOPs for the Polyethylene Pipe Manufacturing Factory

In the **polyethylene pipe manufacturing factory**, SOPs are essential for ensuring that processes on the **extruder lines** are standardized, efficient, and produce high-quality products. The following sections provide detailed examples of how to create SOPs for key processes in the factory.

1. SOP for Extruder Line Setup

This SOP covers the steps required to properly set up the extruder line for polyethylene pipe production. The goal is to ensure that all operators follow the same procedure, reducing variability and minimizing the risk of defects.

Title: Extruder Line Setup for Polyethylene Pipe Production

Purpose:

To ensure that the extruder line is set up correctly, minimizing startup time and ensuring that pipes are produced according to quality standards.

Scope:

Applies to all operators and technicians responsible for setting up the extruder line for polyethylene pipe production.

Responsibilities:

- **Operators**: Follow the step-by-step procedure to ensure the extruder line is set up properly.
- **Supervisors**: Verify that the setup process is followed correctly before production begins.
- **Maintenance Technicians**: Perform any necessary pre-setup maintenance, including checking the temperature control system and die alignment.

Step-by-Step Procedure:

1. **Prepare Materials**: Gather the appropriate die, preheat it, and ensure the raw polyethylene pellets are available and properly stored.
2. **Set Temperature Controls**: Adjust the temperature control system to the required temperature for the type of polyethylene being used (e.g., 220°C for high-density polyethylene).
3. **Install the Die**: Use the quick-change die mechanism to install the preheated die. Ensure the die is aligned and secure.

4. **Test the Setup**: Run a short test of the extruder to verify that the temperature is consistent and that the die is producing pipes with the correct diameter and thickness.
5. **Sign Off**: After verifying that the setup is correct, the operator signs off in the production log, and the supervisor gives final approval for production to begin.

2. SOP for Quality Control on the Extruder Lines

This SOP outlines the specific quality control measures that operators and quality inspectors must follow to ensure that polyethylene pipes meet industry standards.

Title: Quality Control for Polyethylene Pipe Production

Purpose:

To ensure that all polyethylene pipes produced meet quality standards for thickness, strength, and surface finish.

Scope:

Applies to all operators and quality control inspectors responsible for monitoring the production process on the extruder lines.

Step-by-Step Procedure:

1. **Wall Thickness Check**:
   - Every 30 minutes, use a caliper to measure the wall thickness of a pipe sample.
   - The thickness must be within ±0.5 mm of the specified standard (e.g., 3.5 mm for a specific pipe size).
   - Record the results in the quality inspection log.
2. **Surface Inspection**:

- Visually inspect the surface of the pipe for roughness, cracks, or warping.
- If defects are found, stop production and report the issue to the supervisor.
- Document the defect in the production log.
3. **Pressure Testing**:
- Every two hours, test a sample pipe for internal pressure resistance.
- Record the test results, including pass/fail status, and document any corrective actions taken if the pipe fails.

3. SOP for Preventive Maintenance on the Extruder Line

This SOP details the routine maintenance procedures required to keep the extruder line and related equipment in good working condition, ensuring smooth production and reducing downtime.

Title: Preventive Maintenance for Extruder Line Equipment

Purpose:

To ensure that the extruder line and related equipment are maintained regularly, minimizing the risk of breakdowns and ensuring consistent production quality.

Scope:

Applies to all maintenance technicians responsible for performing regular maintenance on the extruder lines.

Step-by-Step Procedure:

Daily Checks:

- Check the extruder's temperature control system for accuracy. Ensure that it maintains the target temperature consistently.
- Inspect the die for any signs of wear or damage and replace if necessary.
- Lubricate moving parts such as the extruder screw and bearings.

2. **Weekly Checks:**
- Perform a full calibration of the temperature control system.
- Check all electrical connections to ensure that sensors are functioning properly.
- Clean the extrusion barrel to prevent buildup of material that could cause defects.

3. **Monthly Checks:**
- Inspect the extruder motor and drive system for any signs of wear.
- Conduct a full inspection of the cooling system and ensure that it is working efficiently.

4. **Record Maintenance:**
- Log each maintenance activity in the maintenance record, noting any issues found and repairs made.
- Ensure that preventive maintenance schedules are followed, and report any delays or missed tasks to the supervisor.

The Benefits of Implementing SOPs in the Factory

1. Improved Product Quality

SOPs ensure that each step of the production process is performed consistently, reducing the likelihood of defects and rework. This leads to higher-quality products and fewer customer complaints.

2. Reduced Training Time

With well-documented SOPs in place, new employees can be trained more quickly and effectively. SOPs provide a clear, step-by-step guide that allows new operators to learn processes faster while maintaining high standards of performance.

3. Increased Efficiency

Standardizing processes through SOPs eliminates variability and reduces the time spent figuring out how to perform tasks. Employees can follow clear instructions, which leads to more efficient operations and fewer errors.

4. Enhanced Safety

SOPs include safety instructions that ensure operators know how to safely handle equipment, reducing the risk of accidents. This is especially important in manufacturing environments where heavy machinery and hazardous materials are involved.

5. Compliance and Accountability

In industries where **regulatory compliance** is essential, SOPs provide the necessary documentation to demonstrate that processes are being followed correctly. SOPs also create accountability, as each step is recorded, and employees are held responsible for following procedures.

Challenges in Developing and Maintaining SOPs

While SOPs offer numerous benefits, there are challenges that organizations may face when developing and maintaining them:

1. Resistance to Change

Employees may resist following SOPs, especially if they are accustomed to performing tasks a certain way. To overcome this, it is essential to involve employees in the development process and explain the benefits of standardization.

2. Keeping SOPs Up to Date

Manufacturing processes can change over time due to new equipment, materials, or technologies. It's important to regularly review and update SOPs to ensure they remain relevant and effective.

3. Balancing Detail with Usability

An SOP that is too detailed may overwhelm employees, while one that is too vague may leave out critical steps. The challenge is to strike the right balance by providing clear, concise instructions that are easy to follow without being overly complicated.

Conclusion: The Role of SOPs in Driving Operational Excellence

Standard Operating Procedures (SOPs) are essential for maintaining **consistency**, **quality**, and **efficiency** in manufacturing. By documenting every step of a process, SOPs ensure that tasks are performed the same way every time, regardless of who is doing them. In the **polyethylene pipe manufacturing factory**, SOPs for extruder line setup, quality control, and maintenance ensure that production is streamlined, defects are minimized, and safety is prioritized.

Effective SOPs provide a foundation for **continuous improvement**, allowing the factory to identify areas for optimization and refinement over time. With clear procedures in place, the factory can maintain high standards of performance, reduce training time, improve product quality, and ensure compliance with industry regulations. SOPs are a critical tool in driving **operational excellence** and ensuring long-term success in manufacturing.

Chapter 15: Kaizen – The Path to Continuous Improvement in Manufacturing

Introduction to Kaizen

Kaizen is a Japanese term that translates to "change for the better" or "continuous improvement." In the context of **Lean manufacturing**, Kaizen refers to the practice of making **small, incremental improvements** to processes, products, or services over time. The philosophy of Kaizen is built on the idea that continuous, ongoing improvements lead to significant gains in **efficiency**, **quality**, and **productivity** in the long term.

Kaizen was popularized by **Toyota** as part of the **Toyota Production System (TPS)** and has since become a cornerstone of **Lean management** worldwide. Kaizen is not limited to large-scale initiatives but focuses on everyday improvements that can be made by all employees, from frontline workers to top management. The principle is that everyone in the organization is responsible for identifying opportunities for improvement and implementing changes.

In this chapter, we will explore the **Kaizen philosophy** and its practical application in a **polyethylene pipe manufacturing factory**. By implementing Kaizen on the **extruder lines**, the factory can create a culture of continuous improvement that drives long-term operational excellence.

The Core Principles of Kaizen

Kaizen is guided by several key principles that define its approach to continuous improvement:

1. Continuous, Incremental Improvements

Kaizen emphasizes making **small, incremental improvements** rather than focusing solely on large, radical changes. Over time, these small improvements add up, leading to significant advancements in productivity, quality, and efficiency.

2. Employee Involvement

A fundamental aspect of Kaizen is that **all employees**—from top management to frontline workers—are encouraged to identify areas for improvement. Kaizen empowers workers by giving them ownership of the improvement process and recognizing their contributions.

3. Elimination of Waste

Kaizen aligns with **Lean manufacturing** principles by focusing on the **elimination of waste** (known as "muda"). Waste can take many forms, such as overproduction, waiting times, defects, excess inventory, and inefficient use of resources.

4. Standardization

Once a process is improved, the new best practices are documented and **standardized** through tools like **Standard Operating Procedures (SOPs)**. This ensures that improvements are sustained over time.

5. Teamwork and Collaboration

Kaizen promotes a culture of **teamwork** and **collaboration**, where employees work together to solve problems and share ideas. Regular team meetings, called **Kaizen events** or **Kaizen blitzes**, are held to focus on specific areas for improvement.

6. Problem-Solving Focus

At the heart of Kaizen is a focus on **problem-solving**. Employees are encouraged to use problem-solving techniques like the **PDCA cycle (Plan-Do-Check-Act)**, the **5 Whys**, and **Root Cause Analysis** to understand the underlying causes of issues and find lasting solutions.

The Kaizen Process: Step-by-Step

Kaizen is a structured approach to **continuous improvement**. The process typically follows these key steps:

1. Identify Opportunities for Improvement

The first step in the Kaizen process is to identify areas where improvements can be made. This may involve reviewing performance data, conducting **Gemba walks** (observing processes directly on the shop floor), or collecting feedback from employees and customers.

Example in the Factory:

On the **extruder lines**, the team identifies that the **high scrap rate** and **long changeover times** are key areas of waste. The team also notes that there are delays in material handling due to disorganized workstations.

2. Analyze the Current Process

Once an improvement opportunity has been identified, the next step is to **analyze the current process** in detail. This may involve mapping out the workflow, gathering data on key performance indicators (KPIs), and identifying specific sources of waste.

Example in the Factory:

The team conducts a **time study** of the die change process on the extruder lines, documenting each step and measuring how long it takes. They also review **scrap rate data** to understand the extent of defects caused by temperature fluctuations during production.

3. Generate Improvement Ideas

In Kaizen, employees are encouraged to generate **improvement ideas** that address the root causes of inefficiencies or problems. This is often done through **brainstorming sessions** or **Kaizen events** where cross-functional teams collaborate to come up with solutions.

Example in the Factory:

The team holds a **Kaizen event** focused on reducing scrap and optimizing changeovers. Some of the ideas proposed include implementing **SMED** (Single-Minute Exchange of Dies) to reduce changeover time, reorganizing workstations using the **5S methodology**, and installing **temperature sensors** to automatically shut down the extruder if the temperature exceeds safe limits.

4. Implement Changes

Once the team agrees on the best improvement ideas, the next step is to **implement the changes**. This might involve updating equipment, reconfiguring workflows, or training employees on new procedures. It's important to start with small, manageable changes that can be quickly tested.

Example in the Factory:

The team begins by implementing **5S** principles to organize the extruder line workstations, ensuring that tools and materials are easy to access. They also install **temperature sensors** to monitor fluctuations and initiate automatic shutdowns if temperatures exceed the set threshold.

5. Measure Results and Evaluate

After the changes have been implemented, it's crucial to **measure the results** to see if the improvements have had the desired effect. This may involve tracking KPIs such as **scrap rate**, **cycle time**, or **overall equipment effectiveness (OEE)**. The team evaluates whether the changes have led to tangible improvements and whether additional adjustments are needed.

Example in the Factory:

After implementing the changes, the team measures the results. The **scrap rate** drops from 12% to 5% within the first month, and die change times are reduced from 45 minutes to 15 minutes. These improvements are recorded and shared with the team.

6. Standardize and Sustain the Improvements

Once the improvements have been tested and proven successful, they are **standardized** and integrated into daily operations. This may involve updating **SOPs**, retraining employees, and putting systems in place to ensure that the improvements are sustained over time.

Example in the Factory:

The team updates the **SOP for die changes** to reflect the new, more efficient process. They also establish a **preventive maintenance schedule** for the temperature sensors to ensure that they continue to function correctly.

7. Repeat the Cycle

Kaizen is a **continuous process**, so the cycle of identifying, analyzing, improving, and standardizing never ends. Each improvement leads to new opportunities for further refinement and optimization, creating a culture of ongoing progress.

Practical Application of Kaizen in the Polyethylene Pipe Manufacturing Factory

Kaizen can be applied to numerous areas in the **polyethylene pipe manufacturing factory** to improve the efficiency of the **extruder lines**, reduce scrap, and enhance quality control. Below are some specific examples of how Kaizen can be used in this context:

1. Reducing Scrap on the Extruder Lines

One of the key challenges the factory faces is a **high scrap rate** caused by **temperature fluctuations** and inconsistent extrusion processes. By applying Kaizen, the team can identify root causes and implement targeted improvements.

Kaizen Approach:

- **Problem Identification**: Operators note that defects such as **brittleness** and **uneven thickness** in the pipes are primarily caused by temperature fluctuations during extrusion.
- **Root Cause Analysis**: Using the **5 Whys** technique, the team determines that the **temperature control system** is malfunctioning because it has not been properly maintained.
- **Kaizen Solution**: The team installs new **temperature sensors** and creates a **preventive maintenance schedule** to ensure that the system is regularly calibrated and checked for issues.

Result: Scrap rates are reduced by 50% within three months, and product quality improves significantly.

2. Optimizing Changeover Times with SMED

Long changeover times during die changes are a source of **downtime** and **inefficiency** on the extruder lines. The team uses **SMED** (Single-Minute Exchange of Dies) as part of their Kaizen efforts to reduce the time required for changeovers.

Kaizen Approach:

- **Problem Identification**: Changeovers are taking an average of 45 minutes, leading to production delays.

- **Root Cause Analysis**: The team conducts a time study and finds that much of the time is spent searching for tools and waiting for dies to heat up.
- **Kaizen Solution**: The team implements **quick-release die mechanisms** and **preheats dies** while the current batch is still running, converting internal setup tasks to external ones.

Result: Changeover times are reduced from 45 minutes to 15 minutes, leading to a 20% increase in production capacity.

3. Improving Material Handling and Inventory Management

Inefficient **material handling** and poor **inventory management** lead to delays and unnecessary transportation waste. By applying Kaizen and using tools like **5S** and **Kanban**, the factory can streamline its material handling processes.

Kaizen Approach:

- **Problem Identification**: Raw materials (polyethylene pellets) are often disorganized, leading to delays in retrieving them for production.
- **Kaizen Solution**: The team implements the **5S methodology** to organize the storage area and uses **Kanban cards** to signal when new materials need to be delivered to the extruder lines.

Result: Material retrieval times are reduced by 30%, and inventory levels are better aligned with production needs, reducing waste.

Kaizen Tools and Techniques

Kaizen relies on several key tools and techniques to drive continuous improvement. These include:

1. PDCA (Plan-Do-Check-Act) Cycle

The **PDCA cycle** is a four-step problem-solving process used in Kaizen to test and implement improvements.

- **Plan**: Identify the problem and develop a plan for improvement.
- **Do**: Implement the change on a small scale.
- **Check**: Measure the results of the change to see if it achieves the desired outcome.
- **Act**: If the change is successful, standardize it. If not, revise the plan and repeat the cycle.

2. 5S Methodology

The **5S methodology** is used to organize and standardize workspaces, making them more efficient and reducing waste. The five steps of 5S are:

- **Sort**: Remove unnecessary items from the workspace.
- **Set in Order**: Organize tools and materials for easy access.
- **Shine**: Clean and maintain the workspace regularly.
- **Standardize**: Establish standards for maintaining organization.
- **Sustain**: Ensure the new system is maintained over time.

3. Gemba Walks

Gemba means "the real place" in Japanese, and **Gemba walks** involve managers and supervisors going to the production floor to observe processes firsthand. This allows them to identify inefficiencies and engage with employees to find improvement opportunities.

4. Root Cause Analysis and 5 Whys

Root cause analysis tools, such as the **5 Whys**, help teams dig deeper into problems to find their root cause. By asking "Why?" five times, teams can go beyond surface-level issues and find lasting solutions.

The Benefits of Implementing Kaizen

The Kaizen approach offers numerous benefits to manufacturing operations, particularly when applied consistently over time:

1. Increased Efficiency

By eliminating waste, streamlining processes, and continuously improving workflows, Kaizen leads to greater operational efficiency. This allows the factory to produce more with the same resources.

2. Enhanced Product Quality

Kaizen emphasizes consistent improvements in **product quality** by identifying and resolving the root causes of defects. This leads to higher **first-pass yields** and fewer customer complaints.

3. Employee Engagement

Kaizen empowers employees to take an active role in identifying and solving problems. This creates a sense of ownership and involvement, leading to higher employee morale and engagement.

4. Reduced Costs

By reducing waste and improving processes, Kaizen helps lower production costs. These savings can be reinvested in the business, contributing to long-term sustainability and growth.

5. Flexibility and Agility

Kaizen promotes a culture of continuous improvement, allowing the factory to quickly adapt to changes in customer demand, new technologies, or market conditions.

Challenges in Implementing Kaizen

While Kaizen offers significant benefits, there are some challenges that organizations may face:

1. Resistance to Change

Employees may be resistant to adopting new processes or ideas, particularly if they have been doing things a certain way for a long time. Overcoming this resistance requires effective communication, training, and involving employees in the Kaizen process.

2. Sustaining Improvements

One of the challenges of Kaizen is ensuring that improvements are sustained over time. Without proper follow-up, the team may revert to old habits, undoing the progress that was made.

3. Resource Constraints

Kaizen requires time and resources to implement. While the focus is on small, incremental changes, it can be difficult to allocate the necessary resources if the team is already stretched thin.

Conclusion: Kaizen as a Tool for Continuous Improvement

Kaizen is more than just a methodology—it is a **philosophy** of continuous improvement that can transform a manufacturing operation. By focusing on **small, incremental changes** and involving **every employee** in the improvement process, Kaizen creates a culture of constant progress. In the **polyethylene pipe manufacturing factory**, applying Kaizen to the **extruder lines** has led to significant improvements in **efficiency, product quality**, and **employee engagement**.

By continuously identifying problems, analyzing processes, implementing improvements, and standardizing new methods, Kaizen ensures that the factory remains competitive and agile in an ever-changing market. The ongoing cycle of improvement is the foundation of **Lean manufacturing**, driving operational excellence and long-term success.

Scenario: Continuous Improvement in Action at Polyethylene Pipe Manufacturing – A Lean Journey

Setting: The **Polyethylene Pipe Manufacturing Factory** is facing challenges with high scrap rates, long changeover times on extruder lines, inefficient workflows, and excessive inventory levels. The plant manager, **John**, is determined to implement Lean manufacturing principles and has decided to launch a comprehensive **Kaizen** initiative that integrates tools like **JIT, SMED, 5S, Kanban, SOPs,** and **PDCA**.

Step 1: Identifying Problems through Gemba Walks

John begins by conducting a series of **Gemba walks**, observing the factory floor to identify inefficiencies and waste. As he walks through the **extruder lines**, he sees several issues:

- **High scrap rate**: Defects such as brittle and uneven pipes are piling up, leading to waste.
- **Long changeover times**: Operators are spending **45 minutes** on each die change, causing significant downtime between batches.
- **Disorganized workstations**: Tools and materials are scattered, making it difficult for operators to find what they need quickly.
- **Excess inventory**: Large stocks of raw materials and finished pipes are taking up space, tying up working capital.

Step 2: Empowering the Team for Kaizen

John calls for a **Kaizen event** and gathers the production team, operators, maintenance technicians, and supervisors in a meeting room to discuss the issues. He explains the **Kaizen philosophy** of **continuous improvement** and emphasizes that everyone will play a role in identifying problems and suggesting solutions. John highlights the **core principles** of Kaizen—**waste reduction**, **employee involvement**, and **incremental improvements**.

"We're not going to make big changes all at once," John says. **"Instead, we're going to make small improvements every day. This way, we can see progress without disrupting our operations."**

He organizes the team into small cross-functional groups, each tasked with identifying specific problems and brainstorming ideas for improvement.

Phase 1: Reducing the Scrap Rate

One team focuses on the **high scrap rate**. Using the **5 Whys** technique, they investigate the root cause of the defects. The team starts with the first why:

- **Why is the scrap rate so high?**
  - Because pipes are brittle and uneven in thickness.
- **Why are the pipes brittle and uneven?**
  - Because the **temperature control system** on the extruder lines is inconsistent.
- **Why is the temperature control system inconsistent?**
  - Because it has not been regularly maintained, leading to temperature fluctuations.
- **Why hasn't it been maintained?**

- Because there is no **preventive maintenance schedule** in place for the temperature control system.
- **Why isn't there a maintenance schedule?**
  - Because maintenance was reactive, only addressing breakdowns after they occurred.

The team determines that the root cause of the high scrap rate is **inconsistent temperature control** due to a lack of preventive maintenance.

Solution:

The team decides to implement a **preventive maintenance schedule** for the temperature control system, as well as installing **new temperature sensors** that will automatically trigger shutdowns if the temperature exceeds the safe range. This will ensure that fluctuations are caught early before defects occur.

Phase 2: Implementing SMED to Reduce Changeover Time

Another group is tasked with reducing the **long changeover times** on the extruder lines. Currently, each die change takes around **45 minutes**, leading to significant downtime. The team decides to apply the **Single-Minute Exchange of Dies (SMED)** method to streamline the process.

Step 1: Separate Internal and External Setup

The team observes the die change process and identifies which steps are **internal** (tasks that must be done while the machine is idle) and **external** (tasks that can be done while the machine is still running). They find that many activities, like **retrieving tools** and **preheating the new dies**, are done after the machine has stopped.

Step 2: Convert Internal Setup to External Setup

The team decides to **preheat the dies** while the current batch is still being produced and **organize tools** at the workstation in advance. This converts much of the internal setup to external setup, significantly reducing downtime.

Step 3: Streamline Internal Setup

The team installs **quick-release mechanisms** on the extruder, allowing the old die to be removed and the new one installed in a matter of minutes.

Result:

After implementing SMED, the team successfully reduces the changeover time from **45 minutes to 15 minutes**. This improvement boosts overall equipment utilization and increases production capacity.

Phase 3: Organizing Workstations with 5S

Another issue identified during the Gemba walks was the **disorganized workstations**, where operators frequently had to search for tools and materials, leading to wasted time and frustration. The team decides to implement the **5S methodology** to improve organization and efficiency.

1. Sort:

The team begins by sorting through the tools and materials at each workstation. They remove any unnecessary items that are not needed for daily operations.

2. Set in Order:

Next, they organize the tools based on usage frequency. Commonly used tools are placed within easy reach, while less frequently used tools are stored neatly but out of the way. Tool shadow boards are installed so operators can quickly see where each tool belongs.

3. Shine:

The workstations are thoroughly cleaned, and the team establishes a regular cleaning schedule to keep the area tidy.

4. Standardize:

The team creates a **standard operating procedure (SOP)** for how tools should be organized and how the workspace should be maintained. This ensures consistency across shifts and reduces the time spent searching for equipment.

5. Sustain:

To ensure that the improvements last, the team implements regular **audits** to check that the workstations remain organized and that the SOPs are being followed.

Result:

After applying 5S, the team reduces the time spent searching for tools by **30%**, leading to smoother operations and more efficient use of time on the extruder lines.

Phase 4: Implementing Just-In-Time (JIT) and Kanban for Inventory Control

Excess inventory was identified as another major issue in the factory. Large quantities of **raw polyethylene pellets** and finished pipes were taking up space, tying up capital, and leading to the risk of overproduction. The team decides to implement **Just-In-Time (JIT) production** to align production more closely with customer demand, reducing excess inventory and waste.

Step 1: Establish Kanban for Raw Materials

To support JIT, the team sets up a **Kanban system** for managing the flow of raw materials. **Kanban cards** are used to signal when new materials should be delivered to the extruder lines, ensuring that polyethylene pellets are replenished only as needed.

- Each extruder line is provided with a set number of Kanban cards that represent the amount of polyethylene pellets required for a specific batch.
- When pellets are used up, the operator sends the Kanban card to the warehouse to trigger a new delivery.

Step 2: Align Production with Demand

The factory shifts from producing large batches of pipes based on forecasts to producing **smaller batches** based on actual customer orders. This reduces the amount of finished goods inventory and ensures that production is directly tied to customer needs.

Step 3: Reduce Overproduction

By aligning production with customer demand and reducing setup times using SMED, the factory can produce smaller batches more efficiently, reducing the risk of overproduction.

Result:

After implementing JIT and Kanban, the factory significantly reduces **raw material inventory** and **finished goods inventory**, freeing up space and lowering costs. The factory now produces only what is needed, when it is needed, resulting in **50% less inventory on hand** and reducing the risk of obsolescence.

Phase 5: Measuring and Sustaining Improvements with PDCA

With improvements in place, John emphasizes the importance of continuously monitoring and sustaining these gains. The team uses the **PDCA cycle (Plan-Do-Check-Act)** to track the effectiveness of the changes and identify new opportunities for improvement.

Plan:

Each Kaizen initiative is carefully planned, with clear goals such as reducing scrap rates, shortening changeover times, and minimizing inventory.

Do:

The team implements the changes, such as installing temperature sensors, applying SMED, and setting up Kanban systems.

Check:

After each improvement, the team **measures results** using key performance indicators (KPIs) like **scrap rate, cycle time, overall equipment effectiveness (OEE)**, and **inventory turnover**. For example, the **scrap rate** is tracked daily to ensure it stays within the new target of 2%.

Act:

If the improvements are successful, they are standardized through **SOPs**. If further adjustments are needed, the team revisits the problem, makes changes, and repeats the cycle.

Conclusion: Transformational Results through Lean Practices

After several months of implementing **Kaizen, JIT, SMED, 5S**, and **Kanban**, the factory sees remarkable improvements:

- **Scrap rate** drops from 12% to 2%.
- **Changeover times** decrease from 45 minutes to 15 minutes.
- **Inventory levels** are reduced by 50%, freeing up space and lowering costs.
- **Employee engagement** improves as workers are empowered to contribute to the continuous improvement process.

- **Product quality** increases due to consistent processes and reduced variability.

John and his team continue to hold regular **Kaizen events**, reviewing performance and identifying new areas for improvement. The **Kaizen culture** has taken root in the factory, driving ongoing success and helping the factory maintain a competitive edge in the marketplace.